Airbrushing for Modellers

Airbrushing For Modellers

by
Richard M. Goldman
and
Murray Rubenstein

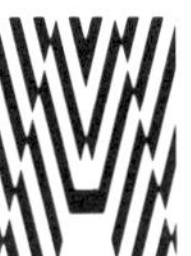

ALMARK PUBLISHING CO. LTD. LONDON.

First published 1974.

ISBN O 85524 1764 (hard cover edition)
ISBN O 85524 1772 (paper covered edition)

Printed in Great Britain by
Davenport Askew & Co. Ltd.,
24 Wates Way,
Mitcham,
Surrey
for the publishers, Almark Publishing Co. Ltd.,
49 Malden Way, New Malden,
Surrey KT3 6EA, England.

CONTENTS

ACKNOWLEDGEMENTS

The authors,publishers would like to thank the following for their help in the preparation of this book: Campaign Colours, Humbrol Ltd., Morris and Ingram Ltd., Rose Paints. Thanks must be extended to all the modellers whose work appears in this book, particularly Bill Quinn who built several models especially for this project, Don Spering and Ralph Laughton.

Front cover top: The body shell of a Ford Cortina Mk.1 shows various techniques of airbrushing incorporated on one model. Stripping tape has been used over a basic colour to achieve the panel stripes. The body was sprayed freehand blue and then black was sprayed on. The headlamp recesses were filled and brush painted. After applying decals, varnish was sprayed on to give an overall sameness to the finish.
Bottom: Each of the polka dots on this B.24 Liberator, used as a rallying plane, was individually airbrushed, using a mask made from a transparent plastic sheet with holes punched in it. The mask was held ¼ inch from the spray surface and the airbrush was directed vertically through the stencil. To ensure a perfect polka dot each time, the dot locations were preplanned and the stencil was cleaned after each application.
Back cover: This HO scale Eggerbahn 0-4-0 tank loco has been airbrushed with "dirt and grime" to achieve a weathered effect. A funnel cover and a ladder have been added to suggest that the loco has been taken out of service.

Introduction

WHY AN AIRBRUSH?

Any serious modeller, that is, one who seeks to reach the pinnacle of excellence known as 'museum standard', has no doubt observed the work of professional modellers in magazines and at exhibitions. With rare exceptions, the top prizes will go to the models which have been airbrushed. This is because airbrushing duplicates the method used to paint the original subject of the model. No matter how skilled the modeller, a truly realistic feather-edged U.S. Navy World War II finish, for example, or a German mottle finish cannot be achieved by hand brushing.

Airbrushing is an art form. With patience, practice and an acquired knowledge of the do's and don'ts, the modeller with talent can produce finished models of a high standard. Once the beginner has produced his first satisfactorily airbrushed model, he will be forever a disciple. There is no match for the smooth, unmarked surface of a sprayed finish.

Caution: Always work in a well-ventilated room with a window open and avoid inhaling paint or thinner fumes.

1: Equipment and Accessories

AIRBRUSHES

The operation of an airbrush is based on a principle of physics known as Bernoulli's Law, which states that the greater the speed of a flowing gas (including air) the lower its pressure. Air under pressure (20 to 40 pounds per square inch) is forced through the body of the airbrush over an opening which is connected to the paint cup. The paint is forced up the connecting tube by the greater pressure on the surface of the paint in the cup (Fig 1). The paint and pressurized air atomize at the juncture of the paint tube hole and the air supply hole.

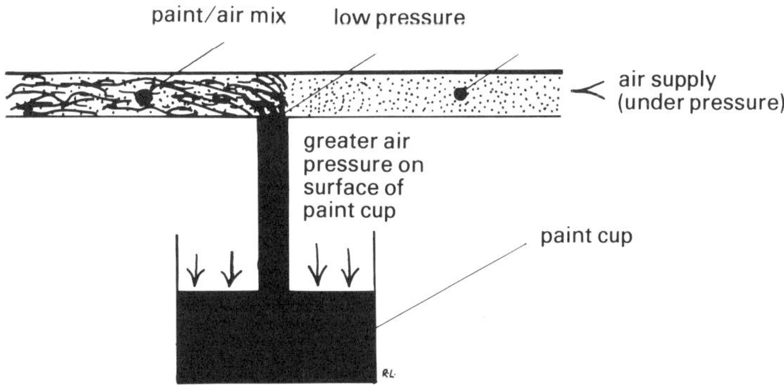

Fig. 1

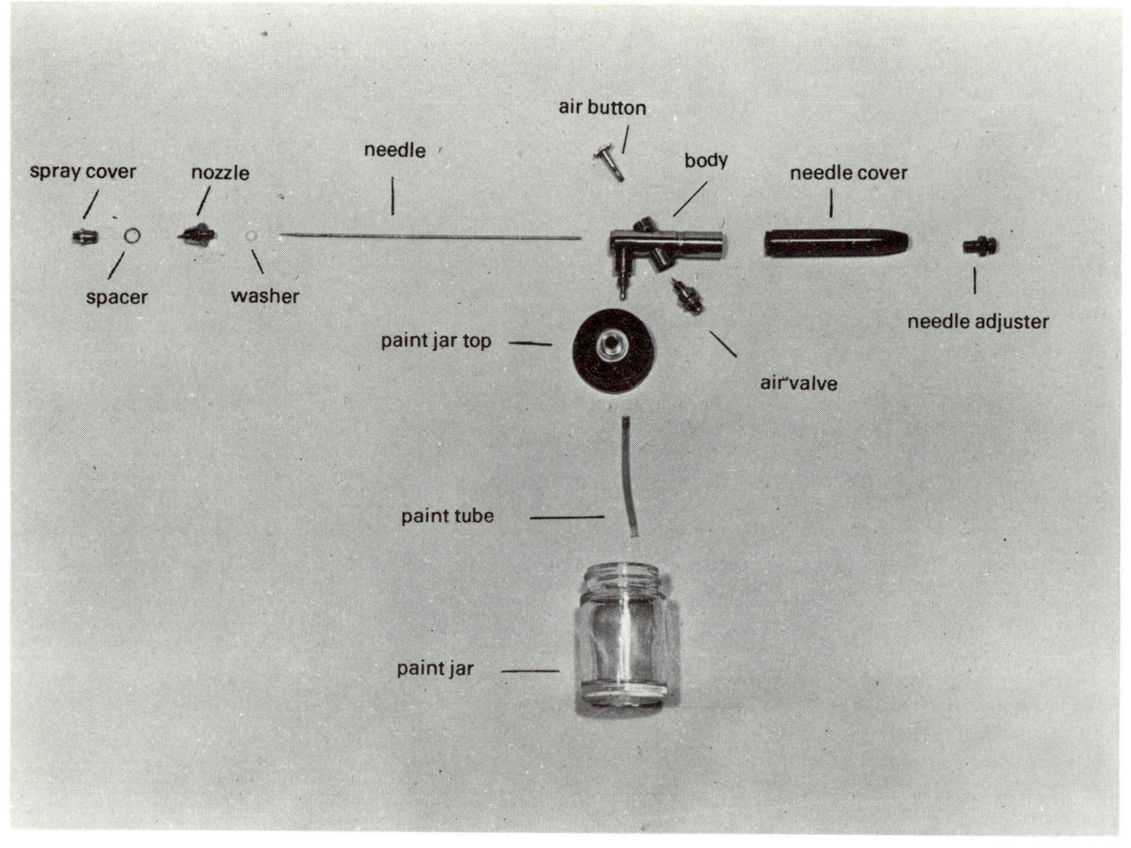

Dismantled single action airbrush

The result is a fine, quick-drying, spray of air and paint (which has been thinned previously to proper consistency). Depending on their quality, airbrushes are capable of producing fine, pencil-thin lines or a coverage of up to several inches wide, by varying the flow of paint and air and the distance from the subject.

Airbrushes are of two types — single action and double action, the distinction being in the manner in which air and paint are allowed to combine. In a single action model the finger presses down on an air control button to open a valve. This allows pressurized air to pass over the paint cup opening, as previously described. The amount of paint is generally controlled by an adjustable knob which moves the paint control tip closer to the air brush tip opening for a finer spray, or further away from the opening for more paint and a wider spray.

A double-action brush is operated by the finger pressing down

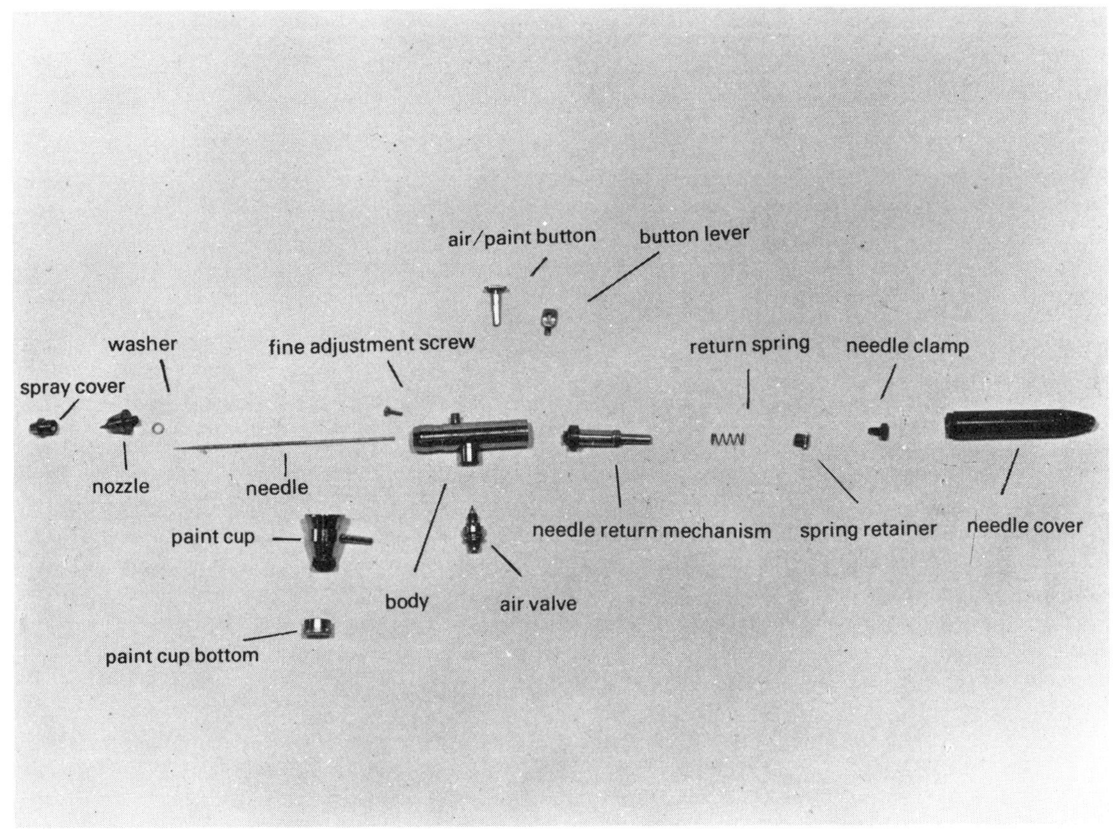

Dismantled double action airbrush

the combination air control button, releasing air, and pulling the paint control spring lever back. The pulling motion draws a paint control needle away from the opening in the airbrush tip and allows paint to flow through, as in a single action brush. The further back the needle is drawn, the greater the opening and the greater the paint flow. The advantage over a single-action brush is the ability to control the release of minute amounts of paint for fine pattern work.

It should be observed that considerably more skill and practice is required to achieve good results with a double-action brush. The price is also somewhat higher. The double-action airbrush has more working parts than the single-action model

The accompanying photographs of dismantled single and double-action models should be studied to familiarize the newcomer with their working parts.

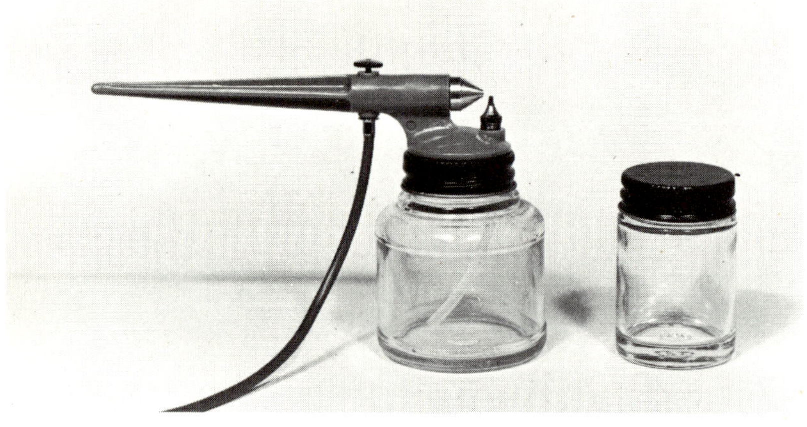

External mix airbrush (Badger 250).

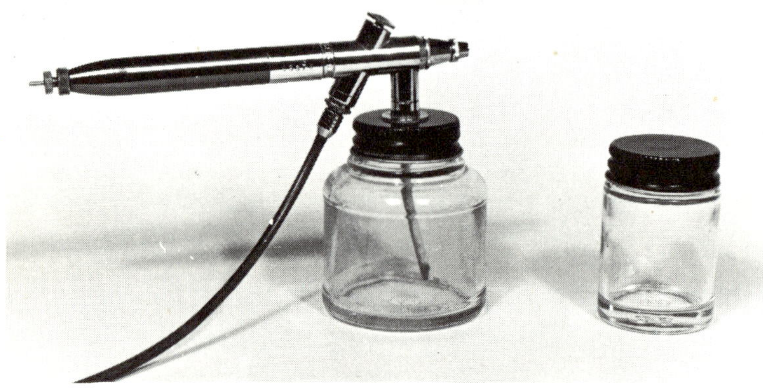

Single action, jar feed airbrush (Badger 200).

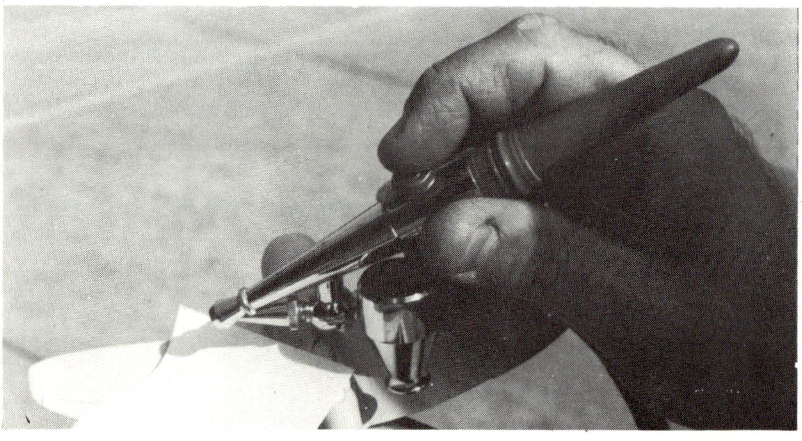

Single action, side cup feed airbrush (Thayer and Chandler).

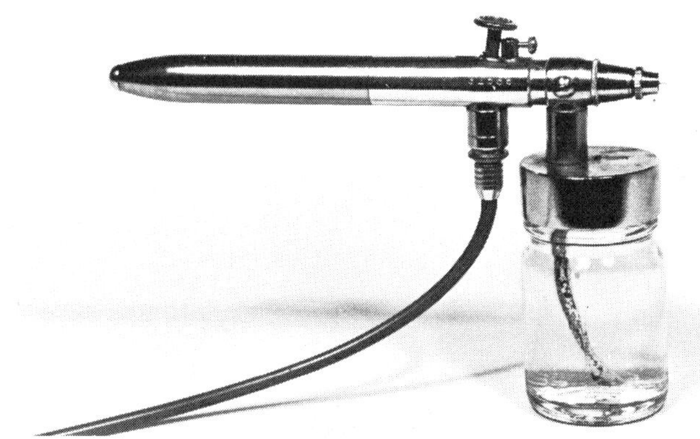

Double action, jar feed, airbrush (Badger 150 IL/XF).

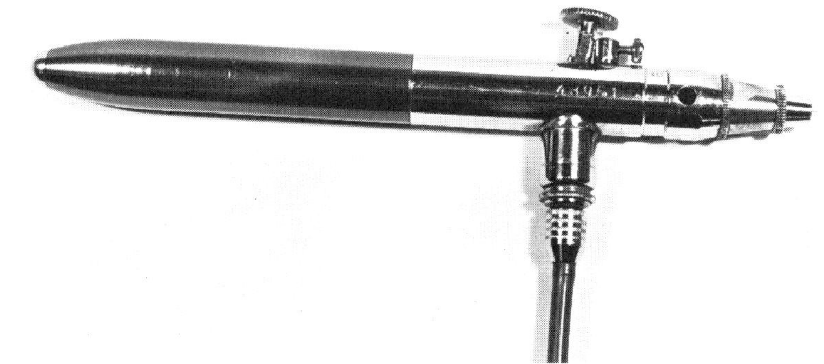

Double action, side cup feed, airbrush (Badger 100 IL/XF).

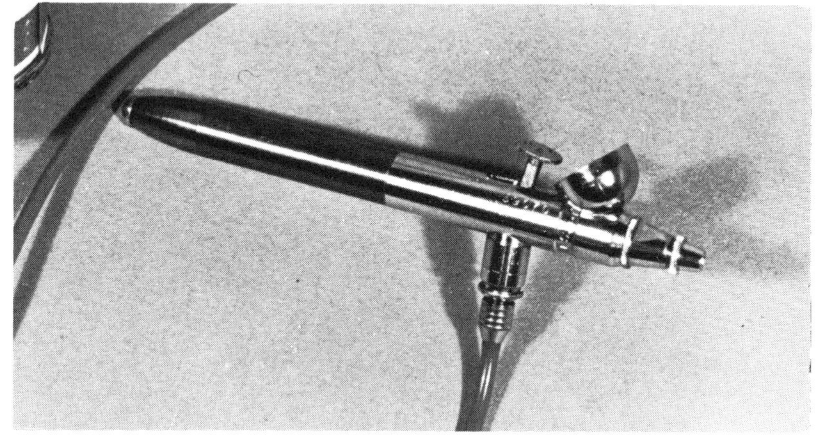

Double action, gravity feed, airbrush (Badger 100 ILG/XFG).

AIR SUPPLY

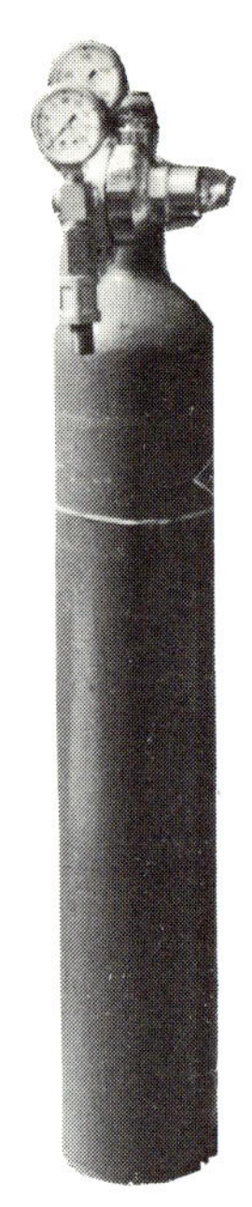

An airbrush requires a supply of pressurized, or compressed, air to operate. The pressure needed will depend on the model, but generally ranges from 20 to 30 pounds per square inch. There are four sources available: compressors, carbon dioxide (CO_2) tanks, aerosol propellant cans and an inflated inner tube using an adapter.

Compressors are the most costly of air sources ranging from a $\frac{1}{10}$H.P., 20 pound pressure unit and a $\frac{1}{4}$ H.P. unit delivering 30 pounds to a $\frac{1}{3}$H.P. commercial compressor for heavy duty work supplying 40 pounds of pressure.

CO_2 cylinder tanks vary in size starting with a small portable ten pound size. They require a gauge and control valve. A ten pound tank will generally give several months of full pressure before replacement. The valve control and pressure gauge allow careful measuring and adjustment of air pressure for the particular work at hand. Moisture problems are minimal.

Recognizing the need for a moderately priced air source, most manufacturers have introduced aerosol cans of propellants to which the air hose may be coupled with an appropriate valve.

Above: CO Tank with fittings.

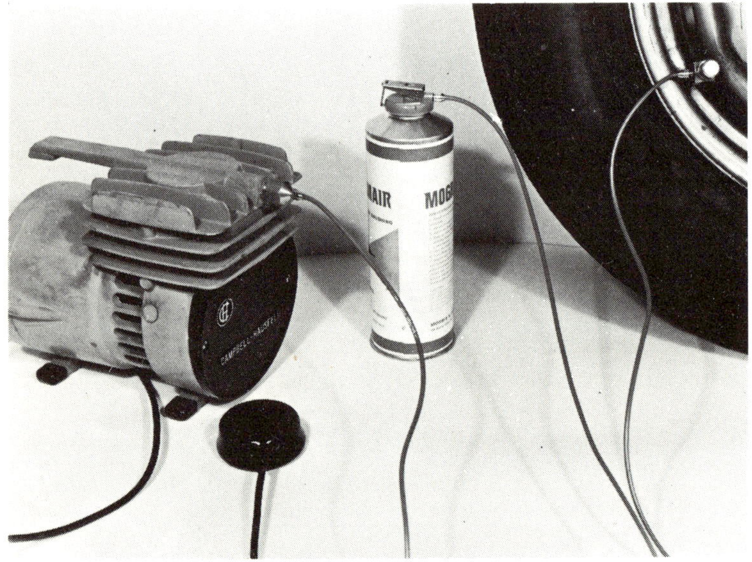

Left: Three types of air supply: Portable compressor and foot switch, 20oz. compressed air can and inflated tyre with tyre adaptor.

ACCESSORIES

If you are working with a compressor in damp conditions you will need a moisture trap to collect droplets of water which may form inside your air hose. The drops have an annoying habit of spraying out with the paint mixture, causing visible drops and spoiling the finish. The trap is cylindrical in shape and fits into a gap cut into the air hose. A small removable screw allows you to shake the water out before use.

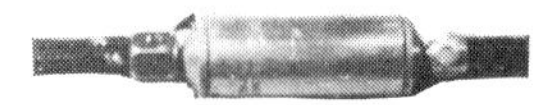

A moisture trap fitted between two halves of an air line.

A portable folding paint spray board approximately 24 inches square can be easily constructed from plywood (Fig 2). Take two square pieces of 24 inch x ½ inch square board and attach them to each other with two hinges on the inside of the edges where the boards meet. Two leather strips or pieces of strong cord can be attached on each side of the board to keep them at a 90° angle. A permanent paint board can be made using the same principle, by adding two triangular side pieces and, if desired, two shelves for paints and tools. A large, deep-edged box top, such as is used for coat or dress boxes, is a handy backboard to stand behind your paint board to catch overspray.

When airbrushing and checking a book or magazine at the same

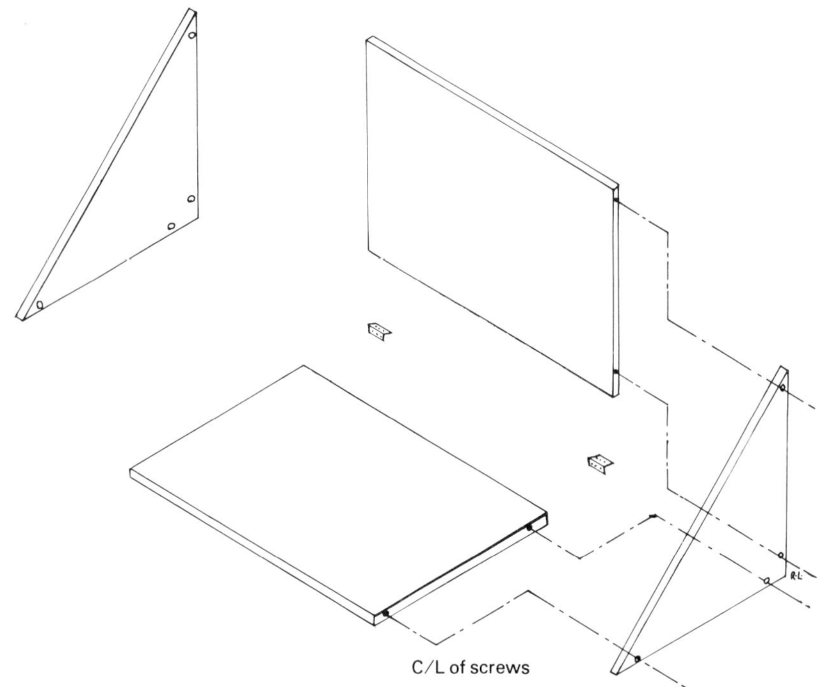

eight screws for optional sides

time, a book rest to hold your book open to a particular page at a proper angle is a convenient aid. Take a piece of scrap ¼ inch or ½ inch plywood 12 inches high (for most books and magazines) and 20 inches wide, and nail a ¾ inch deep strip across the width of the board at the bottom edge, making a lip on which to lean the book or magazine. A 2 inch wide, 10 inch high strip of plywood is attached to the back of the board with a hinge, or a strip of flexible leather. It can then be adjusted forward or backward to support the book rest at a desired angle. Use a strip of leather or sturdy cord attached to the inside of the back strip and the back of the board to keep it from slipping, much as the support for a photograph frame. The book can be held open with a large rubber band or two metal clips.

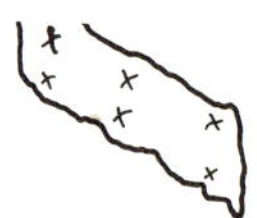

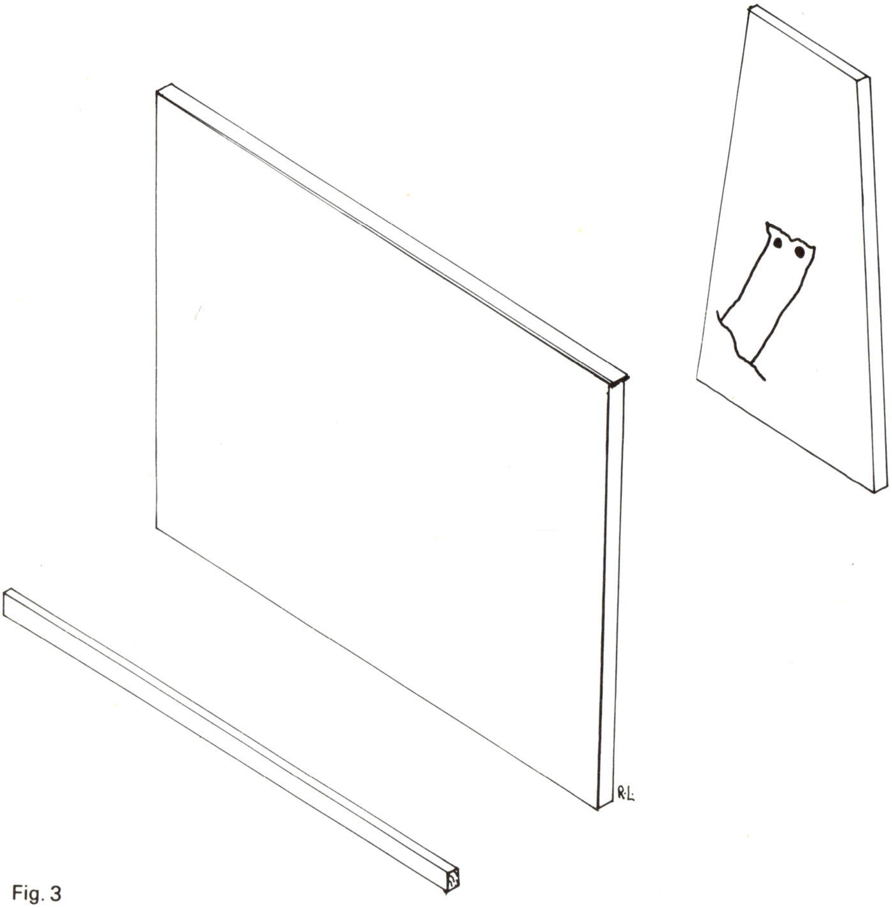

Fig. 3

Every airbrush user has, at times, regretted not having a third hand, particularly when holding a pattern or mask in the left hand and trying to keep a model at the proper spraying angle, with the airbrush in your right hand. Stands made from wire hangers may scratch or damage your model, and the model may not balance at the required angle on a flat surface. A perfect, cost-free device for holding your model at the proper height and angle is a 'no hands' paint box made from a simple shoe box. This will be especially useful for spraying aircraft.

Tape the lid and bottom of the box firmly together. At one end cut out a 3 inch by 2 inch square with a craft knife. Then, remove entirely the other end of the box including the edge of the lid. For spraying the sides of an aircraft fuselage, carefully place

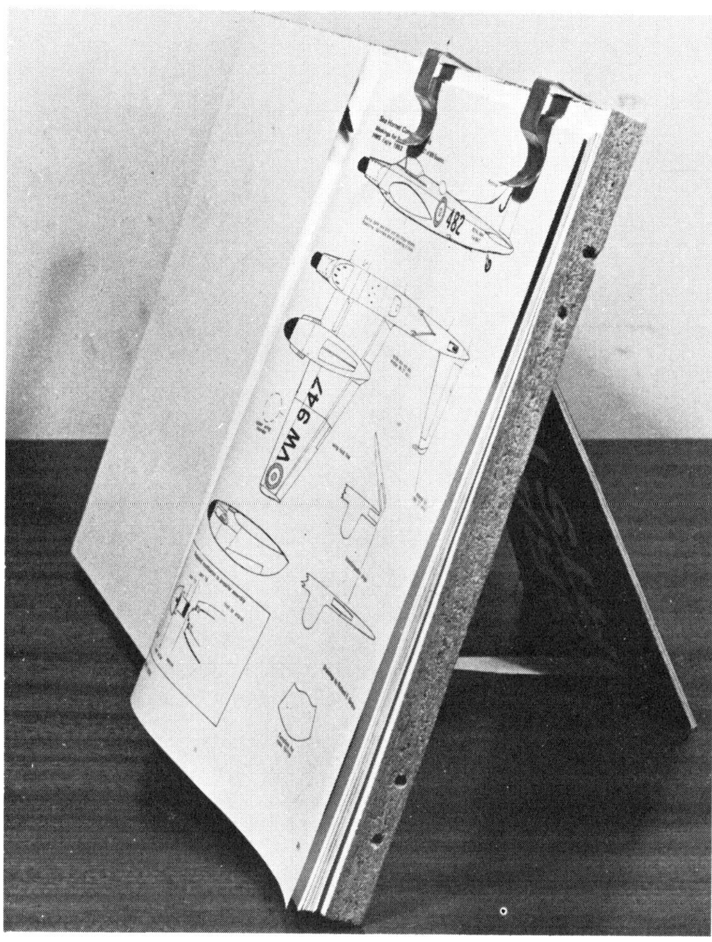

Left: Magazine holder showing rear support and two spring clips holding magazine open.

the wing of the model at the proper spraying angle in the appropriate size opening; the 3 inch by 2 inch hold for single engine aircraft and the open end of the box for multi-engined models. Top surfaces can be sprayed by placing the landing gear in the appropriate size opening, and resting the model on the undersides of the wings. Be careful to clean any wet paint off the box before placing the model in the opening for a respray.

French curves come in various shapes and designs and allow you to trace curved lines which form the outlines for patterns and masks.

A steel ruler is essential for cutting straight edges on masking tape or sheet plastic, without damage to itself or the material to be cut.

Eye droppers are handy for measuring drops of thinners for paint mixing. (Use droppers of the same diameter opening for consistency of measurement).

A magnifying glass is useful to check details of photographs not always evident to the naked eye.

A pair of dividers with a screw adjustment, is an accurate way to check distances without scratching the surface of your model, as with a ruler. Decal placement, for example, is more accurate when checked by dividers.

Tweezers permit decals to be handled gingerly to prevent tearing or folding (stamp tweezers are the best).

A sharp pair of curved ladies' 'cuticle scissors' are excellent for trimming decals and small mask or pattern details.

Small plastic cups are useful to mix paints where you are attempting to mix a colour to a formula. After mixing, pour into your air brush colour cap or jar and discard the plastic mixing cup.

Other accessories, such as masking tapes, cleaning aids, mixing tools, etc, are described in detail in the chapters to follow.

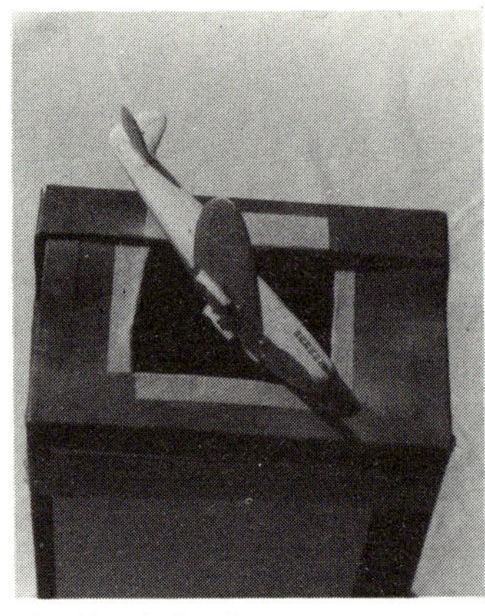

"No Hands Box"

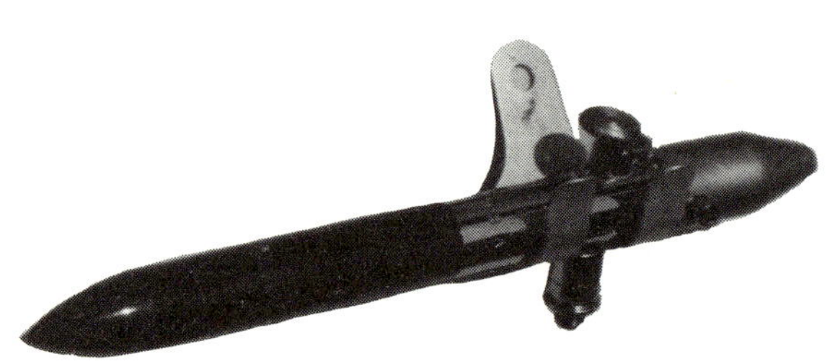

Your airbrush can rest in a holder attached to your work area, even with a full paint cup. Be sure it is firmly in place, and watch for trailing hoses.

2: Researching Your Colours and Finishes

If one word could be used to separate the serious builder of scale plastic miniatures from the equally skilled modeller who builds straight from the box and finishes his project in reasonably matching colours, that word would be, 'research'. A minimal amount of research is essential to make an accurate representation of a real aircraft, A.F.V. or ship, if only to check the accuracy of the kit and recommended colours against a photograph. With the vast amount of research material and sources available very few subjects are inaccessible to the enterprising modeller; many at low, or no cost. Colours, markings and weathered effects cannot be

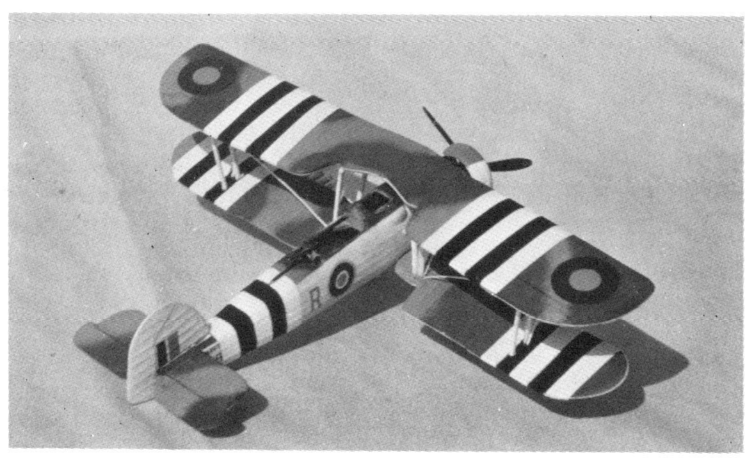

This model of a Fairey Swordfish was the result of a research photograph from the Imperial War Museum.

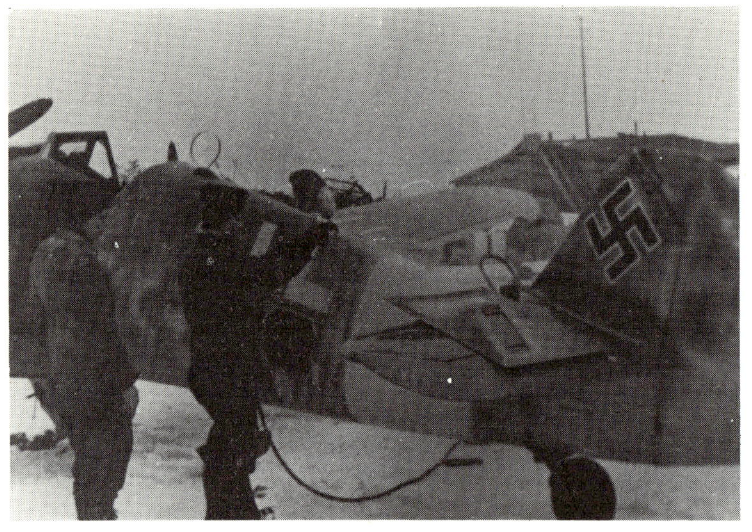

A wartime photograph (taken from a German propaganda magazine) obtained from a fellow modeller (A. Wager).

accurately applied without checking your subject against written and photographic sources.

A particular instance comes to mind regarding a one-of-a-kind model. I was attracted by a photograph in a book of a Fairey Swordfish in D-Day Invasion stripes. The thought of tracing down and modelling what was, by then, a biplane type that had served faithfully since the early 1930's and was still in active combat, was intriguing. Details of colour scheme, stripe placement, armament, a clue to the possible squadron to which it belonged, and a black and white photo, were obtained from the Imperial War Museum (London). A follow-up letter came from the Museum with further, more definite, word on the squadron, which was either No. 833 or 836 of the Fleet Air Arm. This was confirmed by a magazine article listing squadrons using Swordfish during the period. The resulting model was a pleasing one-of-a-kind, with a full history behind it.

Somewhere along the line you may wish to mix a particular colour for which there is no commercial paint; although manufacturers are constantly bringing out new and more diverse colours, much to their credit and the modeller's benefit. Obviously, such mixing cannot be done without reference to a colour chip or paint mixing chart. Trying to get an accurate colour from a description such as 'dark green' or 'light blue' is a virtual impossibility.

Books and magazines are a valuable aid to colour research but the accuracy of colour is dependent entirely on reproduction in printing. Wherever conflict exists, the original chips, rather than printed reproductions, should govern. The same designation

Right: An Imperial War Museum photo reproduced here same size. All I.W.M. photographs carry a reference number to enable the public to order prints. This one carries the number EA 2031/53.

of a particular paint may also vary due to combat conditions, age of paint, 'make-do' colours, etc.

Limited only by the amount of money you wish to spend, your research files can be built up gradually, beginning with newspaper and magazine articles on your particular speciality. Use a scrap-book with dividers or large envelopes appropriately marked, for easy reference later. A file box of 3 inch by 5 inch cards in alphabetical order is handy for jotting notes as to the location of magazine articles and books on a particular subject.

Go to your local library and take notes on books listed in the catalogue which may cover your interest and skim through the books which may be helpful in the future. Browse in second-hand book and magazine shops for inexpensive bargains, being particularly alert for magazines featuring good quality colour photographs. Clip and retain photographs and articles of value, since you will otherwise find yourself with piles of dusty old periodicals, when a page or two is your only interest.

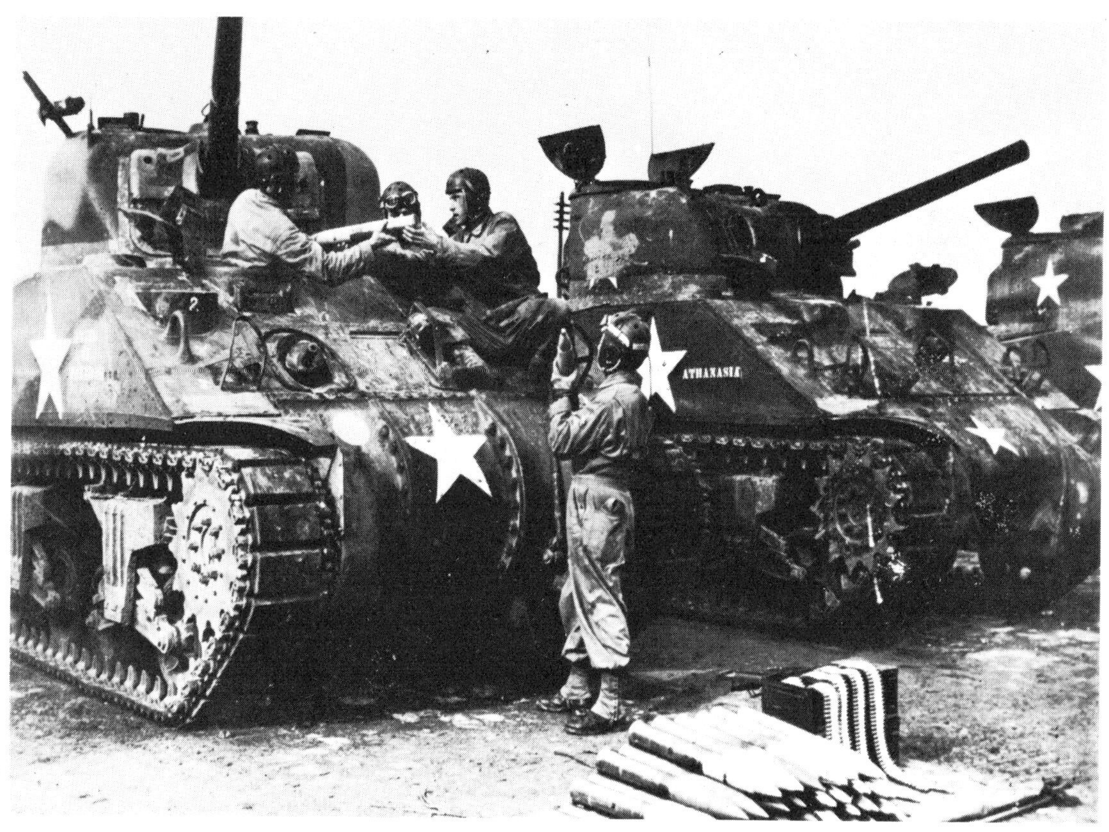

An inexpensive and, of course, authentic source of reference materials and photographs is to be found at military museums and local military and naval bases open to the public. Photography is generally permitted, but check for restrictions. Most military and naval bases which are open to the public encourage photography and opportunities abound to get close-up colour details at small expense. Negatives for copying can then be traded with friends and fellow modellers.

Museums devoted to military matters generally have a stock of printed material for sale. The Wright-Patterson Air Force Base in Dayton, Ohio, the Imperial War Museum in London or the War Museum in Ottowa, Canada, and many smaller museums can provide the modeller with much useful material. Generally, a postcard to a national museum commission (or its equivalent) in your country's capital city will bring forth a list of museums devoted to various subjects. Most government departments are eager to give out information on the location and availability of materials and displays concerning their field.

Further inexpensive reference materials can be obtained from government information services. They are official and accurate and quite detailed. Black and white photographs of excellent quality can, in many cases, be obtained for a little money. Colour photographs are more expensive, however. Public Relations Departments of most manufacturers will generally oblige with a photo or two of a requested aircraft, without charge.

Having obtained all the available free or inexpensive researching aids you can gather, you must turn to somewhat more sophisticated, and costly, items. Excellent research materials can be available through, or exchanged with, fellow modellers in an organised club or society. Highly recommended for any serious modeller is the International Plastic Modellers Society (I.P.M.S.) with worldwide chapters. The cost of membership, which generally includes a sophisticated and up-to-date bimonthly newsletter and quarterly, varies.

As a member, you will be introduced into modelling skills and displays you had only marvelled at in magazines. You can swap information in person, or by mail, with modellers having your interests. New kit information (and those 'juicy' rumours about kits to come) can be exchanged and your latest effort displayed at monthly meetings or contests. Your search for a particular bit of information can be circulated among your fellow members and to other chapters, as well, if you join a local I.P.M.S. group.

Building one's own library of research books can be costly; however, there are many lower priced, but nonetheless accurate, sources. The careful modeller should start with basic materials, as opposed to costly sets of more specialized works.

3: Paints and Thinners

A well known manufacturer of paints for scale modellers has accurately determined that for paint to be in scale, that is, having its thickness reduced to conform to the corresponding size of a 1:72 scale model, a coat of paint should be less than two ten-thousandths (.0002) of an inch thick. All paint contains three ingredients, pigment for colour, a binder made of resin for adhesion to a surface, and a vehicle containing thinners and solvents which make the paint a liquid form. A paint coat of appropriate scale (.0002 inch) can be obtained only by reducing the ingredients to scale, by using finely ground pigments and compatible binders and vehicles. The conclusion is inescapable ... to obtain the best possible results either grind your own pigments and mix your own colours (as some expert modellers do!) or use only paints specifically manufactured for scale models.

Your choice of flat, semi-gloss or gloss paint will, of course, be determined by your prior research. Most photographs will indicate the nature of the finish and literature on the subject of finishes is readily available, as well. A later chapter (Finishing Your Model) will cover this subject in greater detail.

Most modellers using plastic materials prefer enamel based paints to lacquer for coverage and ease of application, as well as the flatness of finish. As a result, the major modelling paints are enamel.

The importance in airbrushing of proper thinners, which are generally turpentine based spirits and which are used to increase the amount of space between particles of paint pigment, cannot be over emphasized. A paint mixture must be of correct consistency for two major reasons: (1) a thick mixture will clog your airbrush and produce splatters and blobs of colour; and (2) a thinned out mixture will not provide good colour coverage or adherence on your model and will have a tendency to be overlong in drying. Care, then, should be taken in your choice and use of thinners. Most of the major paint manufacturers have their own brand of thinner.

MIXING YOUR COLOURS

The key to good airbrushig rests firmly on the consistency of the paint mixture. Splatters, blobs, clogged needles and tips, and a multitude of plagues are caused by a poor mix.

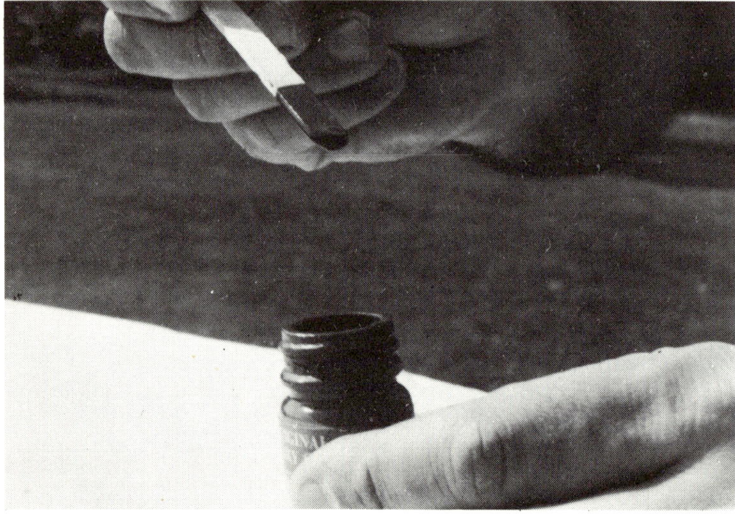

Ice-cream stick being used to test consistency of paint.

The most convenient measure for accurate colour mixing purposes is the 'drop'. Because a drop may vary in size and consistency it is, at best, an approximation, but since a drop is quite small the margin of error is not great. An ounce contains approximately 1200 to 1250 drops of thinner (using a $\frac{1}{16}$ inch opening eye dropper) and a somewhat lesser amount (1100 to 1150 drops) of thinned paint (using an ice cream stick from which the paint is allowed to drop slowly). Such a properly cleaned stick is superior to an eye dropper, which has a tendency to clog with dried colour no matter how many times you clean it with thinner. The size and width, as well as the strength of the stick, make it an ideal paint stirrer as well.

On the subject of stirring, it cannot be too strongly urged that your paints should be well stirred before using. Evaporation of thinners as paint sits in a tin no matter how tightly closed, causes the pigment to harden, so replacement of the thinner and vigorous stirring before each use is a necessity. If your paint contains any lumps or bits of dried pigment, strain the entire contents of the bottle or tin, through a piece of stocking into a clean bottle or plastic cup. Clean the other paint container with a bit of thinner, and replace the paint, minus lumps!

After stirring your paint in the bottle or tin with your paint stick to an even, lumpless consistency which drops slowly from the stick, dip the stick into the paint bottle, allow the first drippings to fall back in the bottle and measure drops into the colour cup of your airbrush. Using an eye dropper (1/16 inch opening) add the correct number of drops of thinner and mix together with your paint stick, being sure that paint and thinner are well stirred. Use only about one-third to one-half of the capacity of your colour cup since a small amount of paint covers a great deal and the likelihood of messy spilling is reduced.

Your mix should now have a consistency which allows it to drop freely from the stick, but not so thin as to drip rapidly. Experiment with your paints until you get the 'feel' of your mixes and the best consistency and drying time for your particular airbrush and technique. Practice with pieces of scrap plastic, which will give you a more accurate and realistic surface, rather than using paper or cardboard. An accurate record on index cards should be kept for later reference on each paint mix, any changes made to it, and any problems encountered. Date your entries so that you can be aware if old paint may be causing a problem. Unused paint can be returned to the bottle providing it has not been mixed with other colours, since the addition of the thinner will not harm the remaining paint in the bottle. Mix your colours using daylight or the light of a natural light bulb or fluorescent tube.

4: Preparing the Model for Painting

Before painting, smooth every join line with fine wet and dry paper; check for raised edges or open gaps; rescribe any panel or rivet lines necessary. Paint tends to accentuate, rather than cover, modelling errors, and a few minutes of extra work will assure that your finish will be mirror perfect.

First, check all join lines by holding up to the light. Any overlap of seams will cast a shadow and should be smoothed again. To

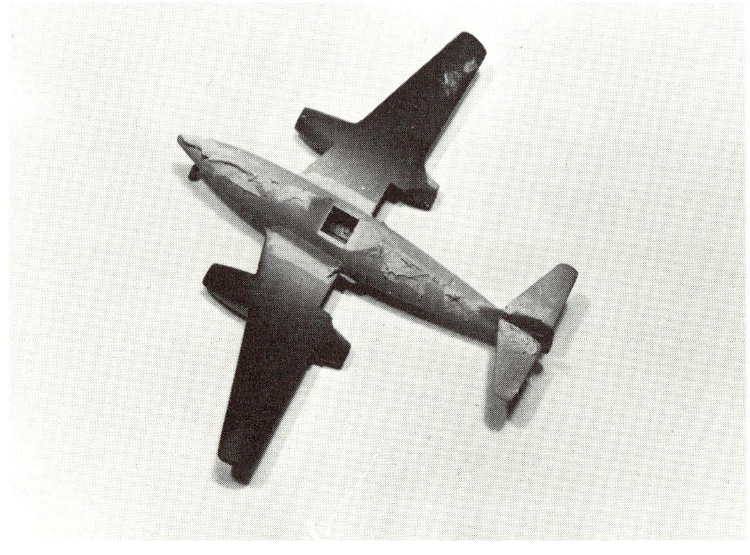

Left: Model with body putty applied to joints awaiting sanding.

ensure smooth joints, brush on flat white paint where components meet and allow to dry before sanding smooth again. The paint will act as a form of body putty to ensure that no minute gaps are visible.

Wedge pieces of paper tissue slightly dampened into recessed areas which require a different colour to prevent overspray. Be sure the tissue does not overlap these areas or you will get colour gaps when spraying. For those modellers who glue on aircraft canopies before painting, a protective cover must be made to prevent painting over. A simple mask made of file card and held in place with a drop of rubber cement, which is easily removable after painting, will do the job quite well. Be sure, though, that your spray is not directed towards the mask but over or away from it, otherwise the fine spray will find its way under the edges of the mask.

Because paint will not adhere well to a surface covered with foreign substances, such as sweat from your fingers, dust, etc., a solution of a few drops of liquid detergent in a cup of water should be prepared. Take a cotton swab, and holding the model by an edge, go over the entire surface, cleaning off all smudges and fingerprints. Drying can be hastened by holding the model near a light bulb, but not too near, as plastic has a low melting point.

All small parts should be laid out on double-sided masking tape for spraying at the same time the undersurface is being done. You may have other models which will use some of the same

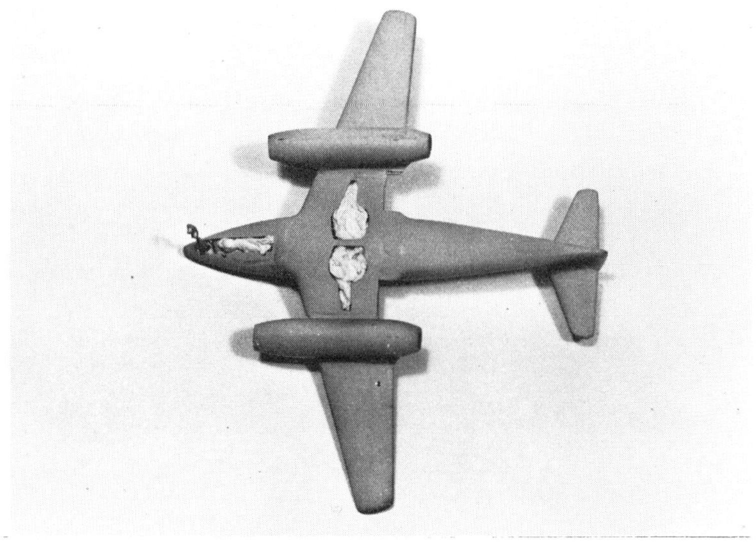

Left: Model with tissue wedged in wheel wells to prevent overspray.

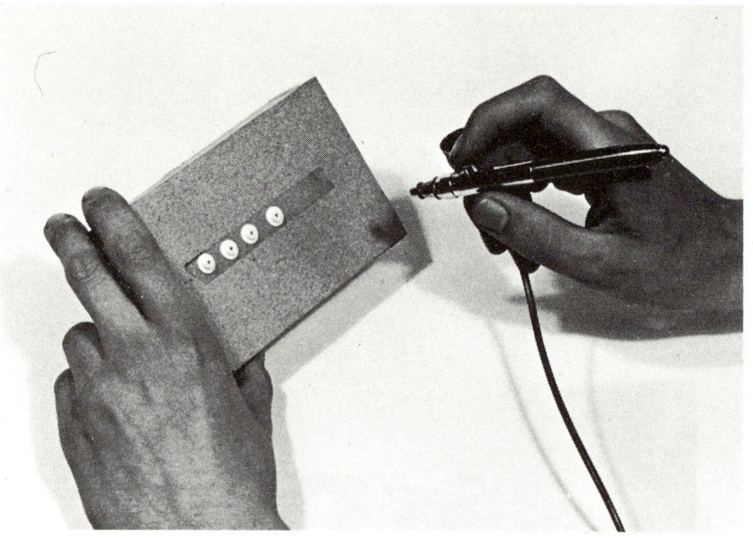

Small parts can be attached to the bottom of a kit box with double sided tape for easy handling when spraying.

colours and these should be prepared for painting at the same time, as well.

Now, you are ready to airbrush. Take care to handle the model by the edges only while painting. Keep the model in a closed box or container while the paint is drying to keep dust off its surfaces. Be especially careful that your paint area is as dust-free as possible, without plastic shavings or filings which may fly up and spoil a newly painted surface.

If you are working with dark material and your scheme calls for a lighter colour, use a spray of grey or another light colour and give a quick coat to the entire model. Allow to dry and give a final light sanding.

5: Masking

Unless you have the steady hand of a professional sign painter, it will be impossible for you to obtain a sharp, straight airbrushed line without help. Even professional airbrush artists use stencils to achieve a crisp finished edge, although freehand work is often used in covering large areas.

While it is possible to freespray models without masking in some instances (one colour models, soft edge demarcations using a raised mask, mottle, etc.) a hard edge can only be achieved by masking off to prevent overspray. The reason is an obvious one — the original subject of the model was normally masked before spraying, or sprayed through or around a template or stencil prepared for that purpose.

The choice of masking materials is varied and preference is generally a personal choice based on trial and error. Transparent tapes are far too sticky, and remove chips of paint even from dry surfaces. They are also difficult to apply because they cannot be easily repositioned.

A personal preference is for a good brand of draftsman's tape which can be applied easily, will stick down well, and lifts without leaving a residue. For sharp lines such as invasion stripes, anti-glare and recognition panels and body bands, flexible pressure-sensitive graphic tape, $^{1}/_{32}$ inch width, available in art stores, combined with masking tape, is excellent for the purpose. Striping tape in $^{1}/_{32}$ inch widths also does the job, providing it is flexible enough to follow compound curves without bunching up. (The choice is endless so long as the tape is *flexible,* because thick, glossy tapes do not bend easily). The method if combining striping tape and masking tape will be described later in the chapter in detail.

In addition to tape, other simple materials, can be used to prevent overspray and to allow paint coverage in a desired pattern. The simplest example is the use of a file card held approximately one inch away from the model (which is set in the 'no hands' paint box) to achieve a soft-edge demarcation. The closer the file card is brought to the model, the sharper the line will appear. Experience will dictate the necessary distance, depending in great part on your particular airbrush. Hold the card in your left hand, parallel to the surface to be airbrushed. With your hand supported on the box edge by a finger or two, airbrush over the edge of the card into the area you are painting. Fog in your feather-edge first and gradually work upward with a mist coat until the top of the area to be painted is reached. On aircraft, take care that lower wings and bottoms of horizontal stabilizers are carefully masked to

Below: Four types of masking. Top left is low-tac masking, top right is Humbrol Liquid mask. Bottom left is stripping tape and bottom right is masking tape.

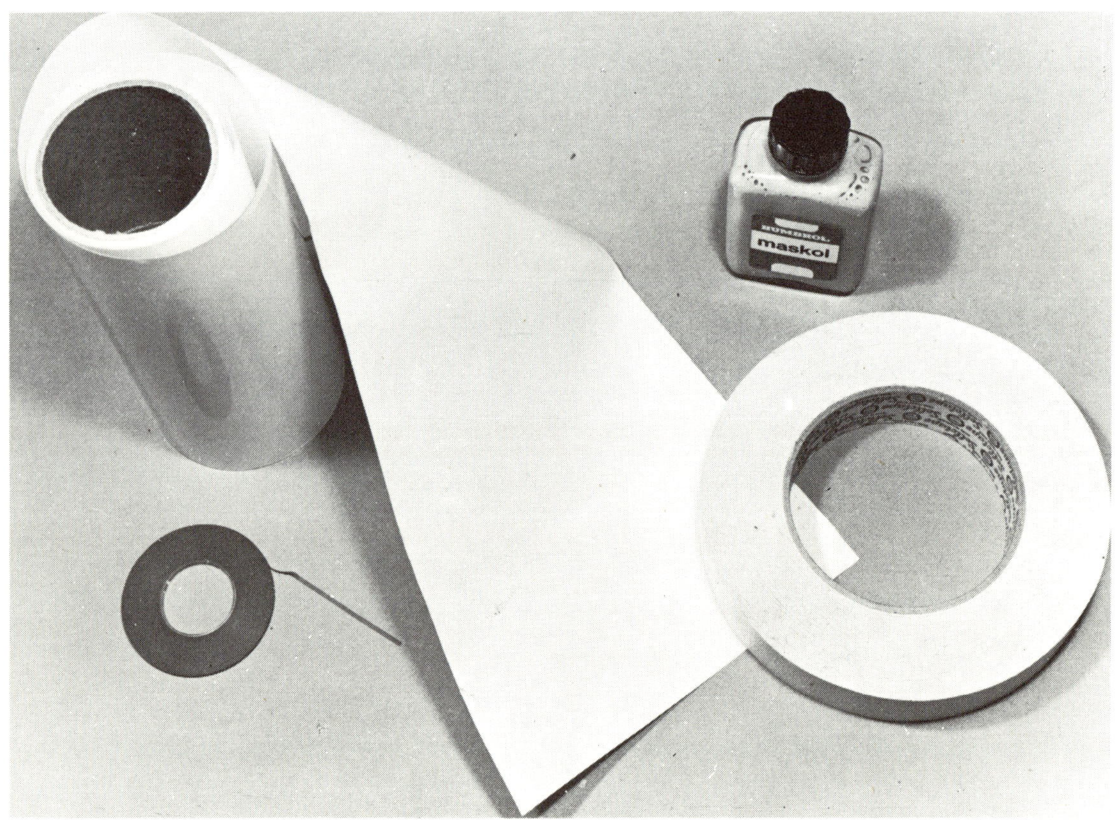

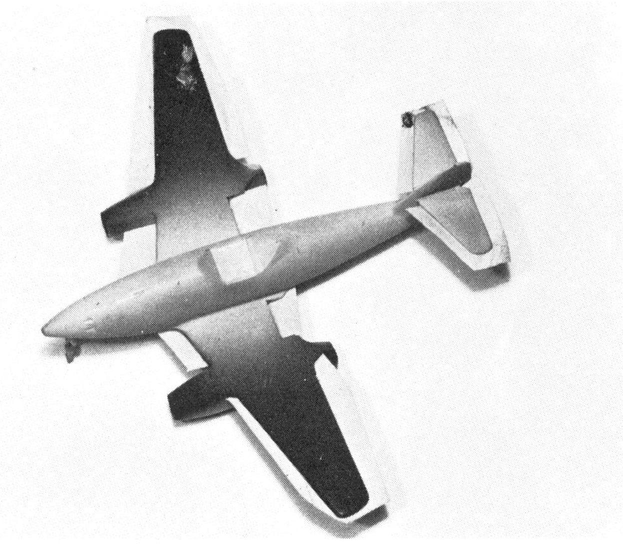

Left: Masking tape under wings to prevent over-spray. Note small square of tape covering cockpit opening.

prevent overspray.

You can now free spray until the proper colour effect and depth is achieved. Stay away from the feather-edge since going over the colour in that area will generally spoil the soft effect you have painstakingly worked for.

Spend a profitable hour of non-modelling by preparing a set of patterns for various camouflage schemes. The British aircraft shadow camouflage schemes of World War 2 for example, as recommended by the Ministry of Aircraft Production, varied with the type of aircraft to be painted. Use photographs of aircraft

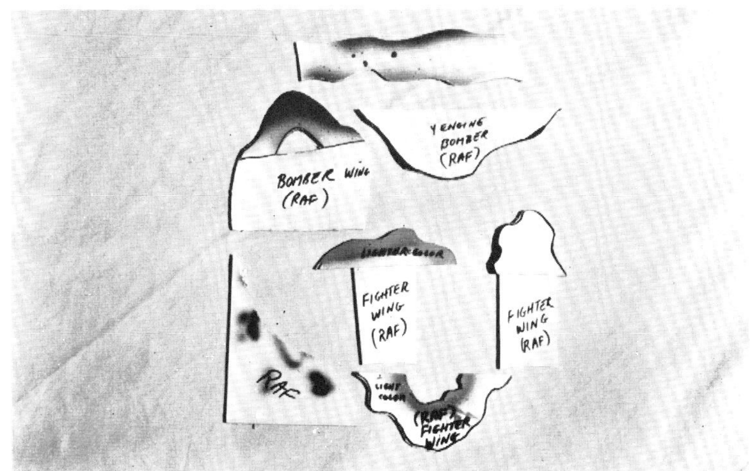

Above: Using a file card as a mask for an aircraft. *Left:* File card masks for R.A.F. World War 2 aircraft. Note holding edges.

to prepare a variety of patterns for other countries.

Using $^{1}/_{16}$ inch thick cardboard or plastic card (thinner material is fragile and has a tendency to bend), draw patterns, freehand or with the aid of a French curve, to match the light colour areas to be protected from paint and cut to shape with a modelling knife or a sharp, curved, pair of scissors. The patterns should be identified in ink for later use (e.g. fighter wing, two engine bomber tail, etc.) and kept in an envelope with a stiff backer to prevent bending.

After spraying the lighter colour hold the pattern over the light area to be masked and spray carefully around it. The closer the pattern is held to the surface while spraying, the sharper the line will appear. Proceed to the next area to be covered and repeat the process, being careful to spray away from light areas. Join up the dark areas of colour with slow, even work to prevent overspraying.

Masking tape cut to pattern will give a hard edge finish where appropriate. After use, remove the tape carefully and preserve it on cardboard for later reference. Free hand airbrushing of soft edge finishes will be discussed in Chapter 6.

Some basics of masking are important to observe at the outset. Never use masking tape as it comes from the roll for it is often nicked or uneven and your paint lines will follow those contours. Instead, lay out the appropriate length on a sheet of flat plastic, glass or metal, keeping it taut. Take a steel rule and a craft knife with a sharp, new blade and carefully cut the masking tape to the proper width. Use the cut edge, which is crisp and unwrinkled, as your painting edge. Stretch the tape slightly and smooth it down with your finger as you apply it to ensure that no paint creeps under the edge.

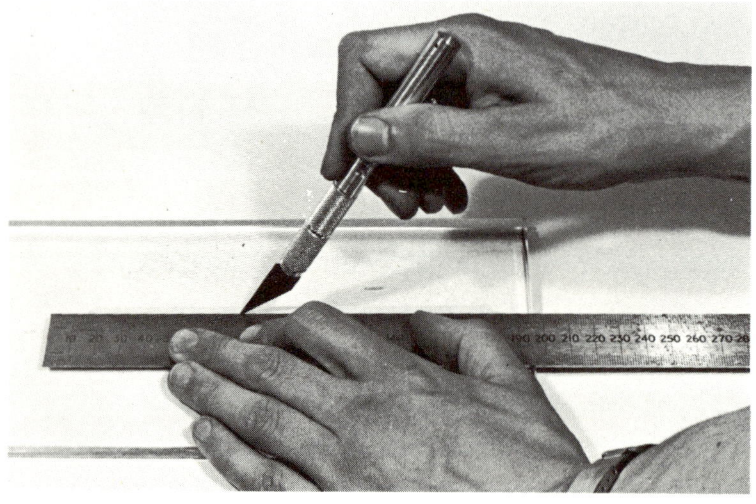

Left: Masking tape should always be laid out on a piece of glass or a tile, and be trimmed with a craft knife to give a straight edge, before being applied to a model.

Be absolutely certain that your base colour is dry before applying masking tape. If not, the base colour will dry on the tape, not the model, and in lifting the tape you will also lift the paint. However, when spraying through, or around, a stencil or pattern which does not touch the model, you can generally begin once the base coat has dried to light touch. Experience will dictate drying time, which is dependent on the make and mix of the paint, humidity in your work area, number of coats applied, etc. Jot down your drying time on a reference card, noting the factors mentioned. The touch-and-go system is a time waste and is unreliable at best, as one learns early on, when repainting becomes necessary to repair damaged areas.

Years ago, a modelling friend, named Don Spering, explained how to take off masking tape to virtually guarantee a sharp, flawless line. As basic as it may sound, you cannot simply pluck tape off and risk chipping but must allow the tape to cut the paint as you lift it. Before your paint dries hard, use a sharp pointed craft knife to lift the end of the masking or striping tape and take a firm grip. Pull the tape back gently but firmly along the line of tape on the model, keeping the lifted tape parallel to the tape being lifted and as close to it as possible. This allows the top strip of tape to act as a cutting edge for the paint which is covering the tape still in place. Work carefully and slowly and the results will be a perfect line each time.

Since straight edge lines are most critically observed and can be used on a wide variety of models, they provide a good starting point for the novice after he has progressed beyond the simple one-colour model. The next logical step is to add contrasting

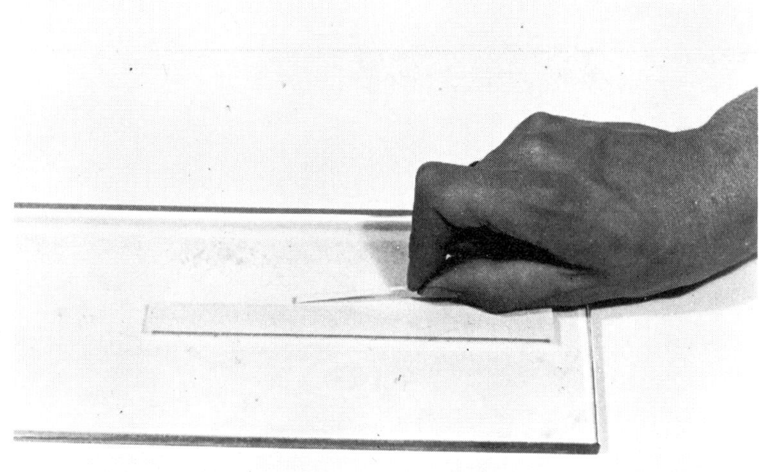

Left: Method of removing masking tape from model, shown here on glass for clarity.

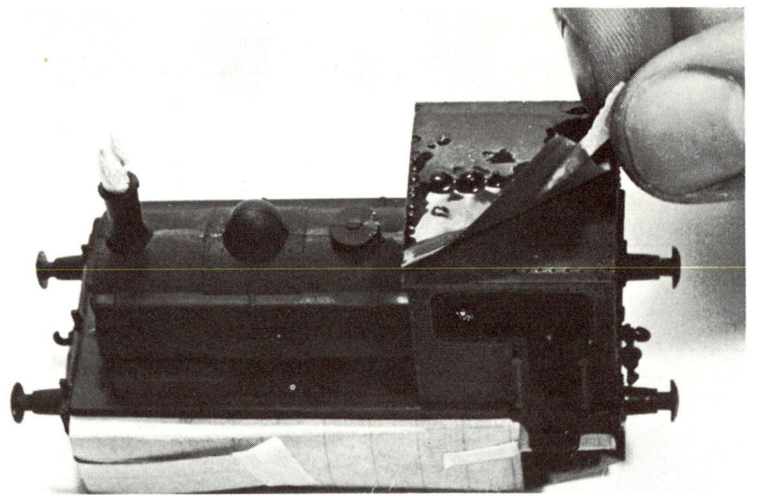

Left: This Airfix 0-4-0 saddle tank Loco shows three types of mask. In the funnel is a piece of tissue to prevent the inside of the funnel being sprayed. The running gear is protected by file card and the roof has a coating of liquid mask. Note the piece of tape on the corner of the liquid mask to make lifting easier.

colour using a basic masking principle which will be followed in various forms, throughout all your straight work.

Airbrushing World War 2 D-Day invasion and other identification stripes, such as the alternating yellow and black of British aircraft in the 1956 Suez campaign, follows a similar but somewhat more complicated process. First check your reference sources to ascertain the number and colour of the stripes. For the most part, D-Day stripes were three white and two black alternating, but examples of three black and three white have been seen on certain two-engined aircraft and four narrow black and three wider white stripes shown on Hawker Tempest and Typhoon aircraft. The stripes were generally equal in width and were not less than 18 inches wide and began approximately six inches inboard of the national emblem. Scaled down to model size, each stripe would not be less than ¼ inch on 1:72 scale aircraft, ⅜ inch on 1:48 scale aircraft, ¾ inch on 1:24 scale aircraft. Thus, on a 1:72 scale model an area 1¼ inches wide on each wing, above and below, should be masked off firmly with striping or chart tape and masking tape combination and sprayed white. Several coats may be necessary, rather than a single heavy application. Spray into the area to be painted but not into the tape edge where the paint can creep under the tape edging or pile up, leaving an unsightly ridge. Allow to dry completely, leaving tape on the model. Carefully cut two strips of masking tape ¼ inch wide for 1:72 scale aircraft or the wider stripes for larger scale aircraft from a wide roll to ensure two sharply cut sides to each strip.

Measure ¼ inch from the inside edge of the masked off panel

on wing and fuselage and apply 1/32 inch striping tape. Apply the ¼ inch masking tape strip on, but not over, the edge of the striping tape. This covers one white stripe. Repeat the process from opposite panel edge for second white stripe. Measure ¼ inch from inside edge of first white stripe and apply 1/32 inch striping tape. Measure ¼ inch from inside edge of second white stripe and apply 1/32 inch tape. Firmly place ¼ inch wide masking tape on, but not over, the edges of the striping tape. This is the third white stripe and the uncovered areas are the two black stripes. Spray and allow to dry fully. Carefully remove masking tape and striping tape as previously detailed and you will have a super striping job that will enhance any model.

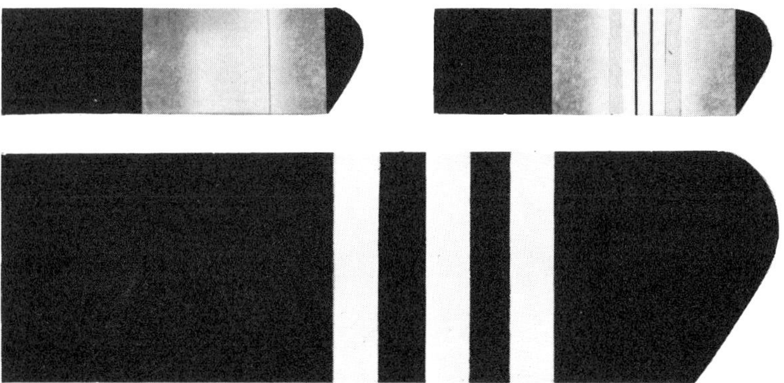

Top left: The outer edges of the area of three white and two black stripes are measured off and masked with stripping and draftsman's tape for sharp edges, and airbrushed white. *Top right:* The three white stripes are masked off so that the two black stripes can be airbrushed. The area between the two centre stripes of black tape will be covered with draftsman's tape. *Bottom:* The finished wing shows crisp hard edges of colour.

The next step in the progression of masking is to move from straight edges to curved or irregular demarcation lines. These masked edges are generally hard lines but sharper soft line effects can be achieved as well by not bringing the airbrush spray as close to the tape as for hard edging.

Camouflage patterns ranging from World War 2 aircraft to modern jet aircraft can be accurately reproduced with the judicious use of masking. Spray the model with the lighter colour and after establishing your pattern from reference sources, take a piece of draftsman's masking tape of sufficient width to allow you to trace the outline of the part of the model you wish to paint. Use two or more overlapping pieces, if need be, although two inch wide tape is sufficient for most 1:72 scale models. Cut away the excess tape and draw in your camouflage pattern, using a French curve if necessary. Crosshatch the area that you will not paint (the lighter colour). With a sharp pointed craft knife, carefully cut out the crosshatched areas on the tape and firmly apply them to the model, in the proper position, pressing all edges down. It should be noted that the tape masking off the upper and lower

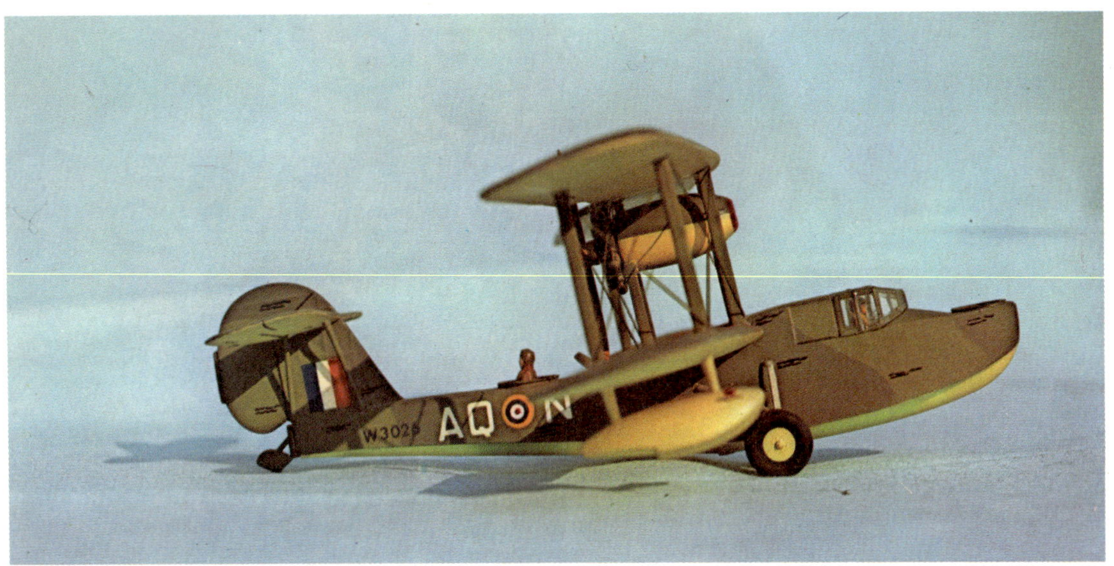

Above: A Coastal Command Walrus. The factory finish is soon to be eroded by salt water and hard use (Model by Don Spering).

Below: An 0-6-2 Narrow Gauge, freelance, loco in dark green industrial trim with red oxide cab roof (anti rust). Note the well weathered look of the running gear (Model by Ralph Laughton).

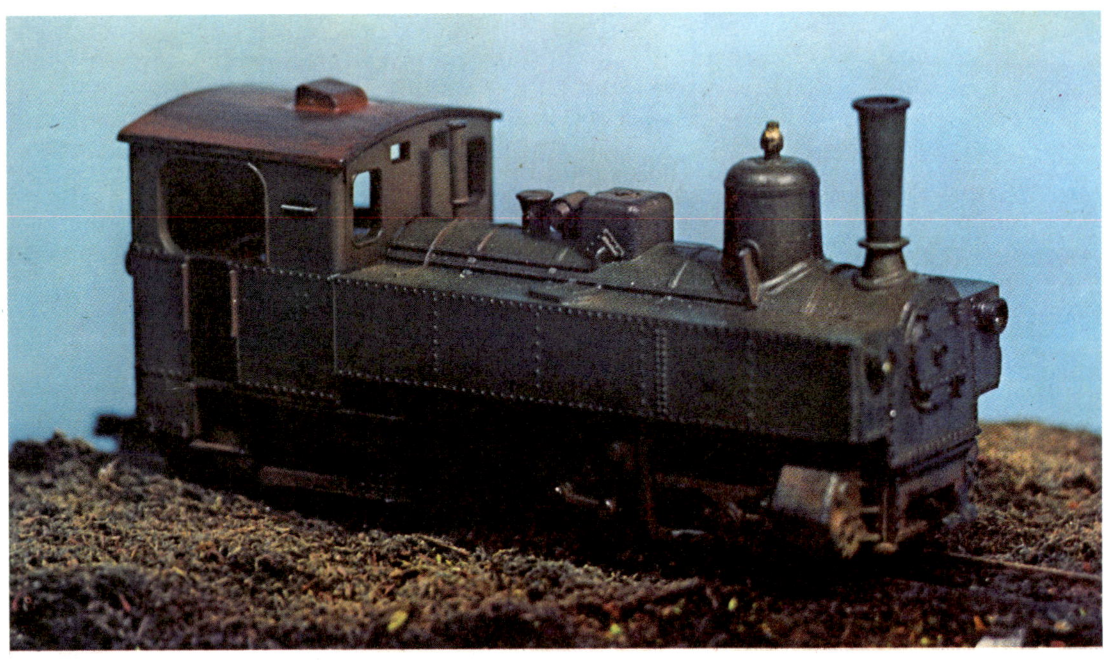

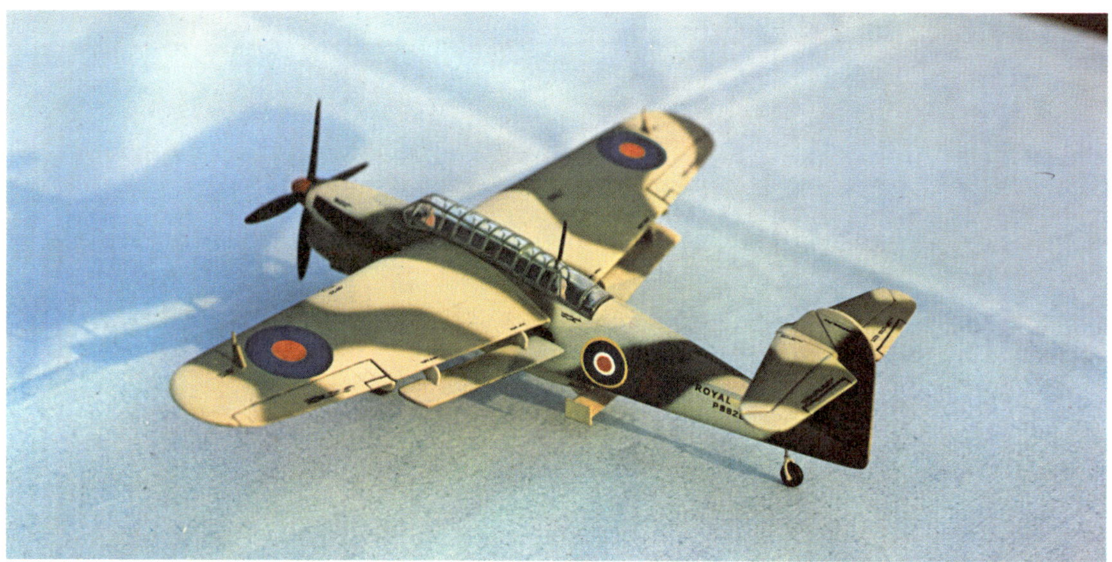

Above: A Royal Navy Barracuda in a Sea Grey and dark green feathered pattern camouflage (Model by Don Spering).

Below: An airbrush can be used on buildings, such as this booking hall, to apply a surface of dust, grime and moss without obscuring the original colour (Model by Ralph Laughton).

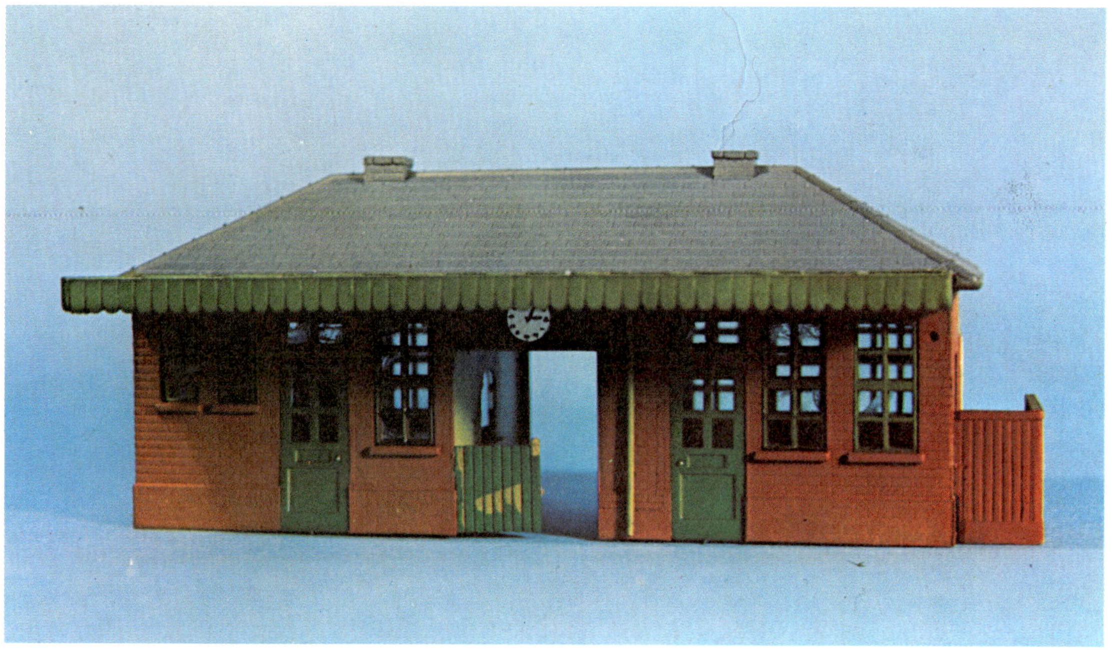

colour lines is left in place after spraying the lighter colour. This prevents overspray when the darker camouflage colours are applied.

Spray cautiously *into* the areas to be painted but take care not to spray into the tape edges. Work slowly and use several light coats rather than attempting to cover in a single heavy coat. If a softer edge is desired, permit the areas closest to the tape edges to remain slightly lighter in colour. Allow to dry and remove the masking tape carefully with a knife point and tweezers. The results, after some experience, should be most pleasing.

Some modellers prefer this method for straight line German splinter camouflage, using sharply cut masking tape firmly pressed onto the model. Both methods have been used with equally good results, but experience will dictate your own preference.

Several World War 2 aircraft present an interesting "wobbly" line demarcation between upper and lower fuselage colour. The Japanese were partial to this scheme, but it can also be found on R.A.F. bombers, such as the Wellington and on some American types. To achieve the effect, place a strip of masking tape on a cutting sheet and measure the length of the aircraft fuselage, cutting off the balance of the tape. Draw the line using a felt pen and carefully cut along the line with the point of a craft knife. Lift off the portion which will serve as the mask and press firmly on to the fuselage, being careful to flatten the edges of the tape. Use the other portion of the tape for the opposite side of the fuselage.

Spray the colour over the top of the tape into the area to be painted. If a softer edge is desired keep the spray further from the masked edge and conversely, bring the spray closer to the tape if a harder line is sought. After drying, carefully remove the tape as previously described. The result is a particularly interesting one and not difficult to achieve.

To achieve varied shades and textures on silver or aluminium aircraft, mask off panels in certain areas (as per photographic references). Spray these panels with a different brand of silver paint from the base coat silver. The effect will relieve the 'sameness' of the overall silver colour and will provide a realistic appearance.

Many modellers have found a great deal of difficulty in painting perfectly straight canopy braces, particularly on 1:72 scale model aircraft. Some modellers who use vacuum formed canopies, as well as those using canopies from the box, have adopted the method of cutting $\frac{1}{32}$ inch stripes of masking tape, or using $\frac{1}{32}$ or $\frac{1}{64}$ inch striping tape, laid firmly on a plastic or metal cutting board. They then airbrush the tape when spraying the appropriate top colour, right on the cutting sheet (clean up time later). After a short drying time the strips are lifted with the tip of a craft knife and applied as braces to the vacuum formed canopy, or the original canopy with the braces carefully sanded down (and scratches polished with a dab of toothpaste). The result is as realistic, or more so, than painting braces on canopies, since real aircraft have actual braces, not painted lines, on their canopies.

On aircraft larger than 1:72 scale, mask off your canopy panels before the canopy is glued to the model and body putty is applied. Mask with a clear tape, scoring the tape on both sides of the braces and lifting the scored portions, leave the panels covered (press down gently). Airbrush the canopy braces and fuselage at the same time. Allow to dry and carefully remove the masking with the point of a craft knife. Properly done, your canopy braces should be crisp and straight, although a bit of touching up may be necessary with a good sable brush and a toothpick dipped in thinner.

The painting of a one-of-a-kind insignia on an individual aircraft, World War 2 Allied bombers being prime examples, provides for an interesting use of masking. Often there are decals for the purpose but a particular nose marking may have caught your fancy and the only option is to draw your own, or to use the following method.

The key is to find a drawing or replica in approximately the same scale as your aircraft, since the emblem can be trimmed somewhat smaller or somewhat larger, following the same outline. Photocopy the emblem, or draw the emblem freehand yourself. Place a piece of masking tape of sufficient size to contain the emblem on a piece of wax paper to prevent curling and sticking, and glue the photocopy of the emblem, trimmed to approximate outline, to the masking tape. With a fine pointed pair of fingernail scissors, start inside the emblem and carefully cut the shape of the emblem until you are left with a stencil outline. Remove the wax paper, taking care not to tear the masking tape and apply the masking stencil to the aircraft, pressing the edges down firmly. Airbrush the predominant colour and let dry. Keeping the stencil in place to prevent overpainting, lightly draw in the next most prominent feature and paint in carefully by hand. Complete the remaining details and allow to dry to a hard finish. Spray with a protective coating to prevent chipping or flaking.

As a modeller gains experience, less and less dependence on masking is needed, but even professional modellers are unable to achieve with freehand airbrushing what has been achieved on the full sized aircraft with masking or stencils. Experiment with different techniques and materials until you feel comfortable, and confident, as you work.

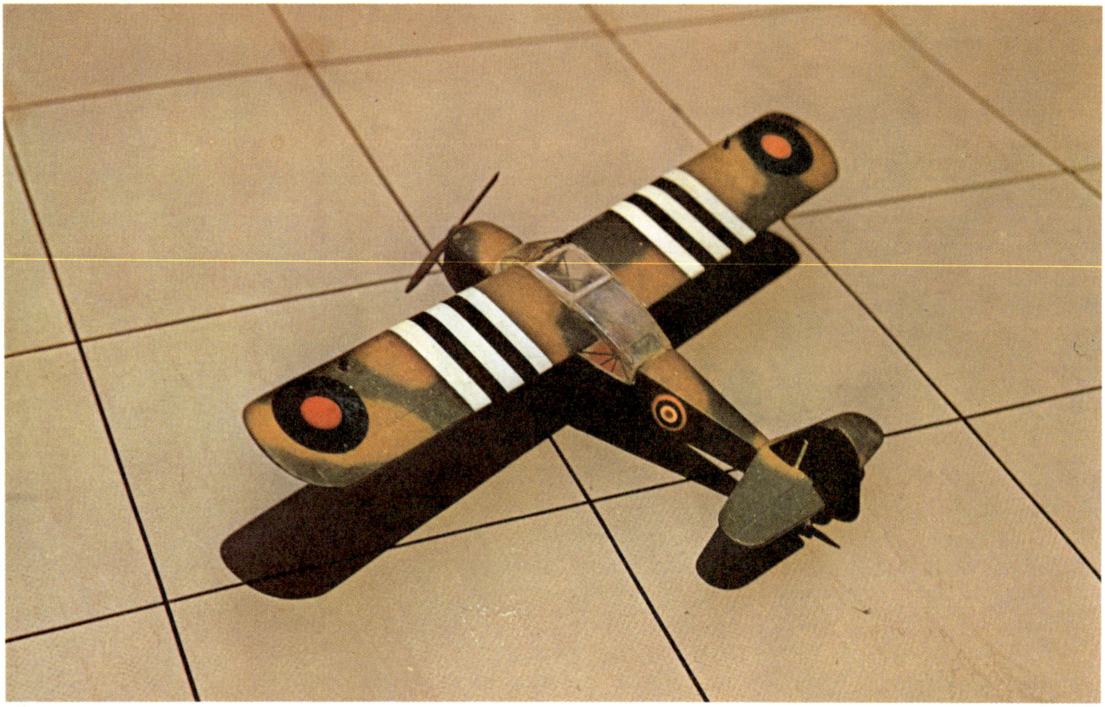

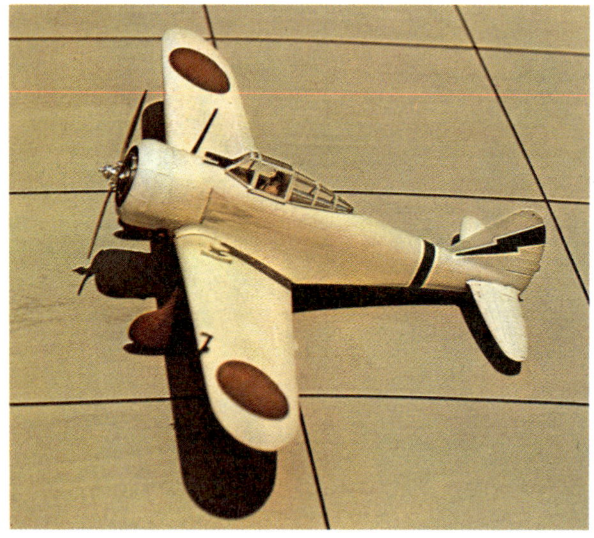

Above: An Auster A.O.P. shows crisp invasion stripes against a sand and spinach R.A.F. camouflage scheme. (Model by Bill Quinn).
Left: All markings were masked and airbrushed (no decals) on this pre-World War 2 Japanese Ki21 "Nate". (Model by Bill Quinn).

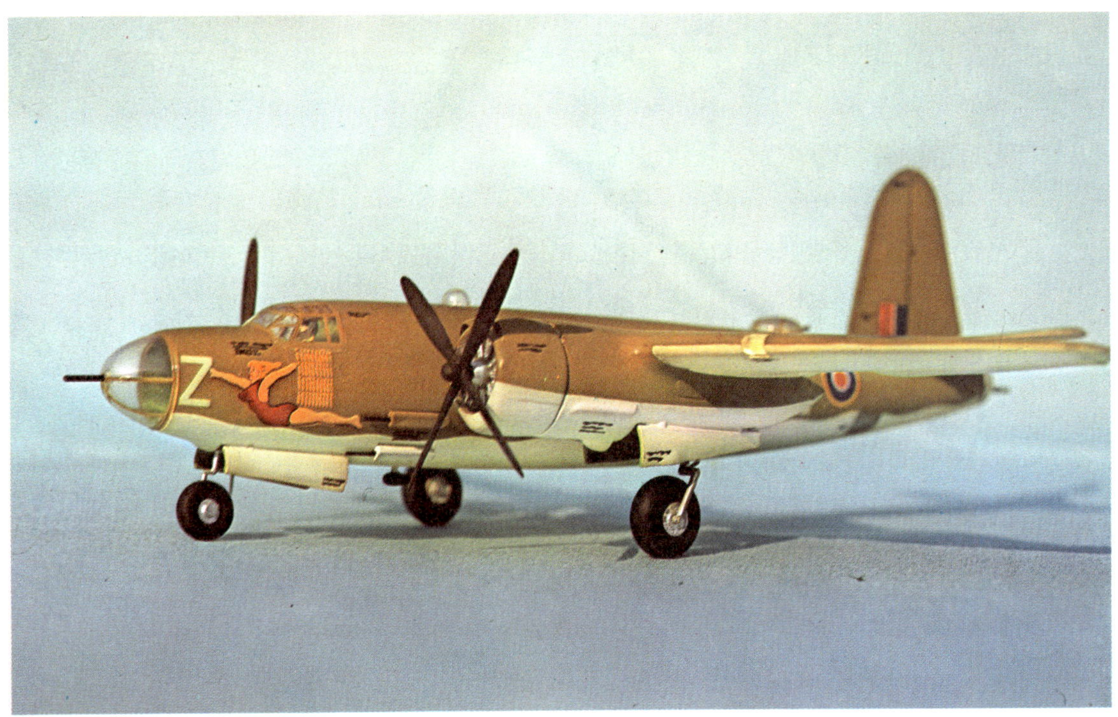

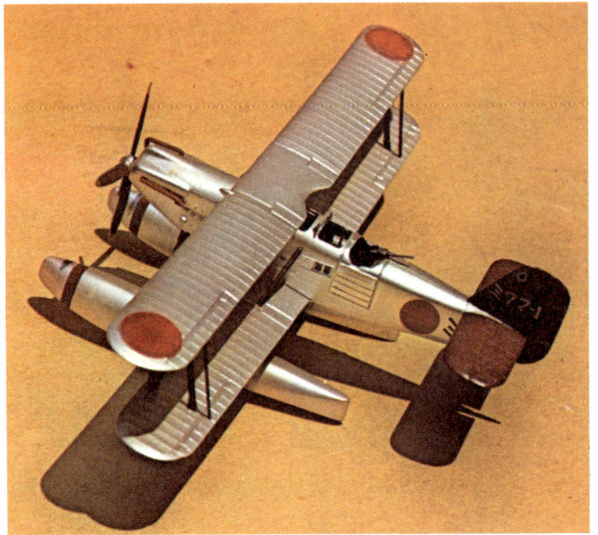

Above: A South African Air Force Marauder II shows a "pin up" emblem airbrushed as described in the text. (Model by Don Spering).
Right: A Kawanishi "Alf" in the pre-1914 Japanese Navy scheme of overall silver with blood red tail surface. (Model by Bill Quinn).

6: Airbrushing Techniques

AIR SUPPLY

Whether you decide upon a compressor, a CO_2 tank, aerosol propellant can or an inflated tyre (Chapter 1), be sure that the hose connection is only finger tight. Never tighten with a wrench or a pair of pliers which will strip the thread of your hose fitting. If air is escaping around the fitting, check for stripped threads, loose connection or damaged washer.

Finger tighten your airbrush to the hose connection and open your air supply valve or turn on your compressor. If you are using a pressure indicator, set it for between 25 and 30 pounds. Before putting your colour cup on, spray air through the brush and check for any leaks at connecting points. Open the turnscrew to your moisture trap, if you are using one, and blow out any moisture which may have gathered. If all is in order, you are ready to paint.

HOLDING THE AIRBRUSH

After mixing your paint and attaching the colour cup firmly into the colour hole, the airbrush should be held like a pen, using the fore finger to press down on the air pressure button. The hose should rest over the back of the hand so that it falls away from the tip of the airbrush. Some modellers prefer to take an extra turn of hose around their wrist, but it is a matter of personal comfort. The other hand is used to adjust the colour supply knob or nut, whichever is used on your brand of airbrush and can be varied as you

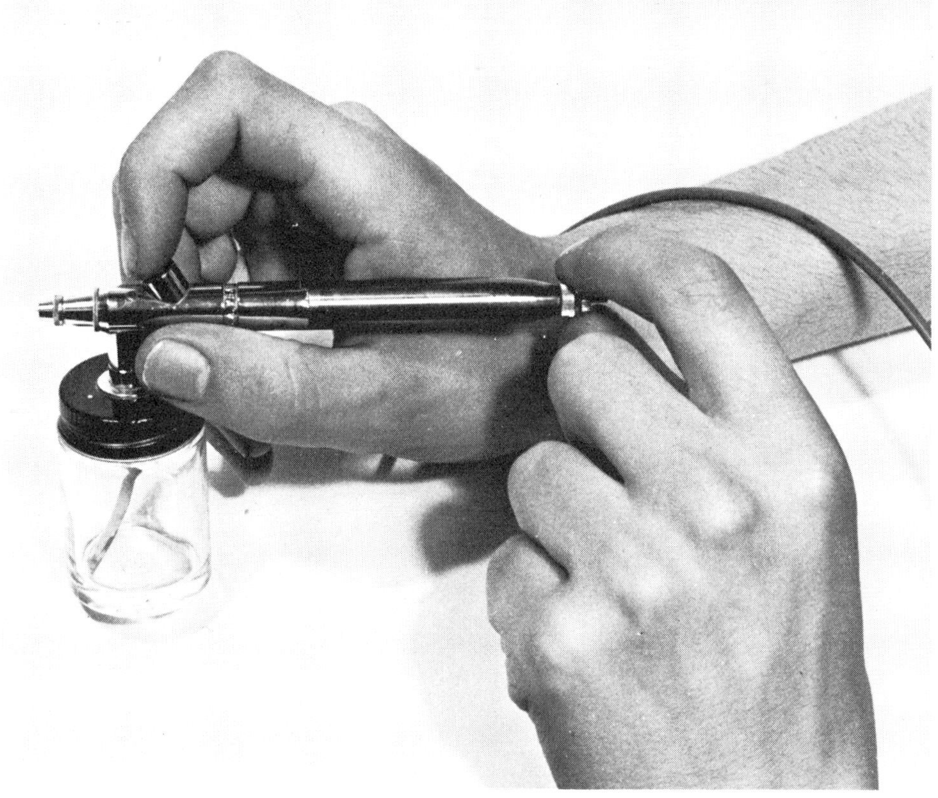

Holding a single action airbrush

are spraying. As often occurs, your left hand will be holding the model (when the 'no hands' box is not being used) and it will be necessary to first adjust your spray to a desired position, for each change will necessitate your putting the model down, and using your left hand to make the colour adjustment.

Paint stands and model holding devices are quite useful for overall spraying, but a firmer base is necessary for extreme close-up work. A bit of imagination and ingenuity will provide the modeller with the holder which best suits him.

The portion of the index finger to be used on the air supply button is also a matter of 'feel'. Some prefer the tip of the finger (particularly with a double action brush which requires more touch) and others prefer the pressure to be applied by the bend between the first and second joints. Experiment until you feel at ease with the brush and use the position which affords you the most control.

If using a single-action airbrush, hold it at a right angle to the model. Starting at a point beyond the paint surface to prevent

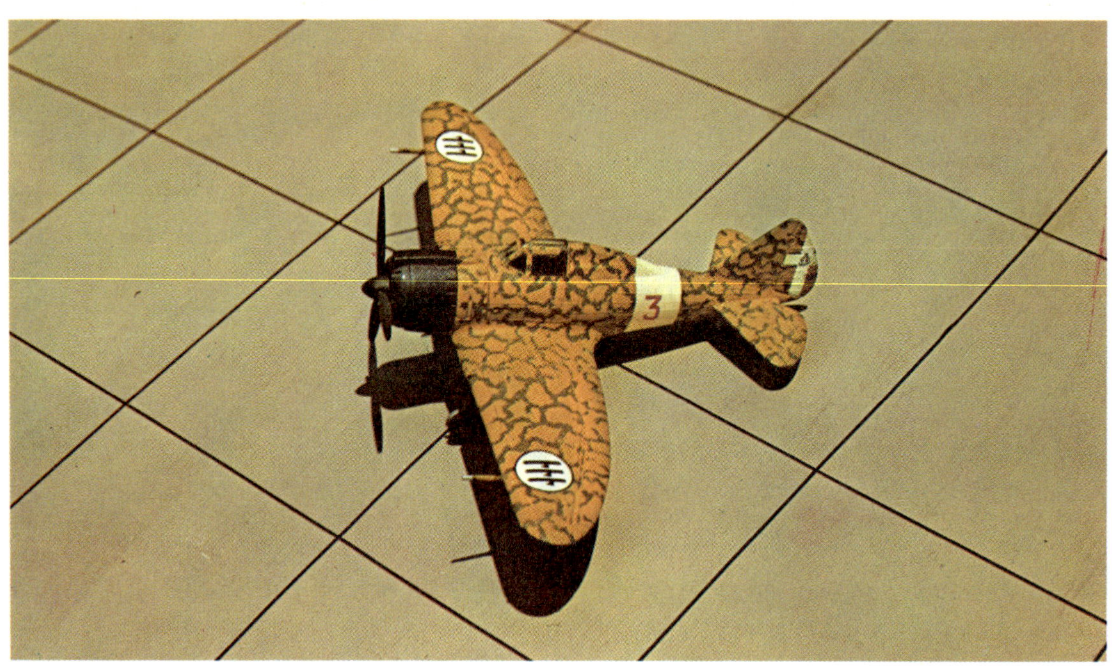

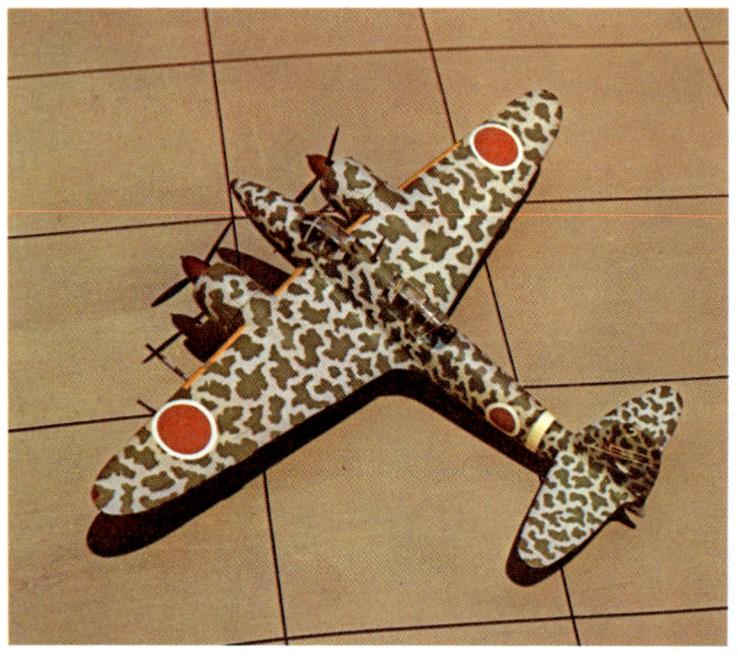

Above: Liquid mask was used to "draw" the sand blotches over the light green upper surfaces of this Reggionne RE 2002 (Model by Bill Quinn). *Left:* A kawasaki Toryu "Nick". Shows a veined pattern used by the Japanese in 1943. (Model by Bill Quinn).

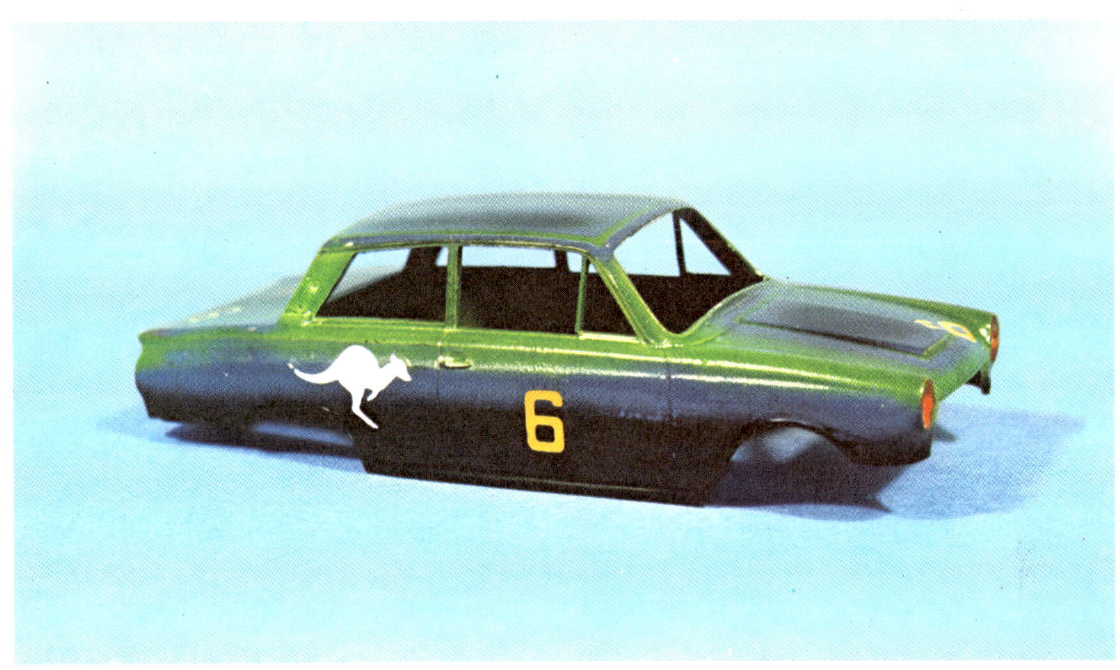

Above: The body shell of a Ford Cortina Mk.1 shows various techniques of airbrushing incorporated on one model. Stripping tape has been used over a basic colour to achieve the panel stripes. The body was sprayed freehand blue and then black was sprayed on. The headlamp recesses were filled and brush painted. After applying decals, varnish was sprayed on to give an overall sameness to the finish.
Right: This HO scale Eggerbahn 0-4-0-tank loco has been airbrushed with "dirt and grime" to achieve a weathered effect. A funnel cover and a ladder have been added to suggest that the loco has been taken out of service.

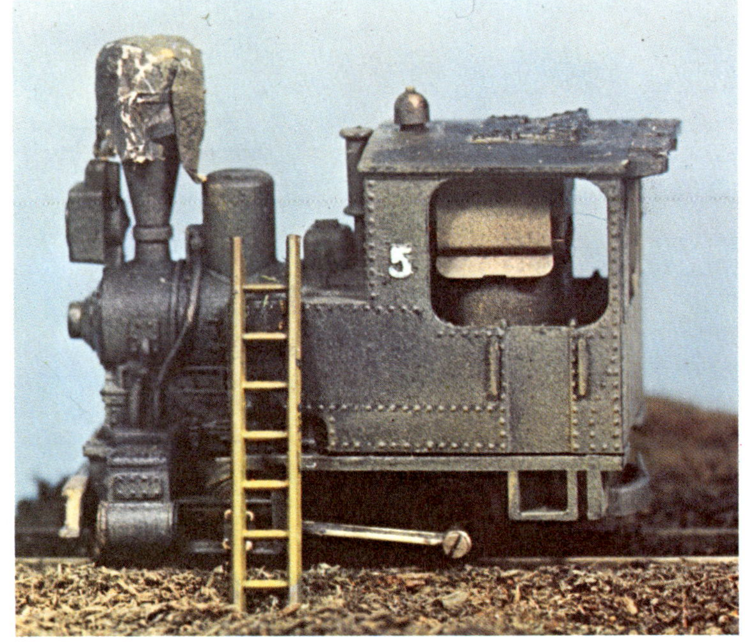

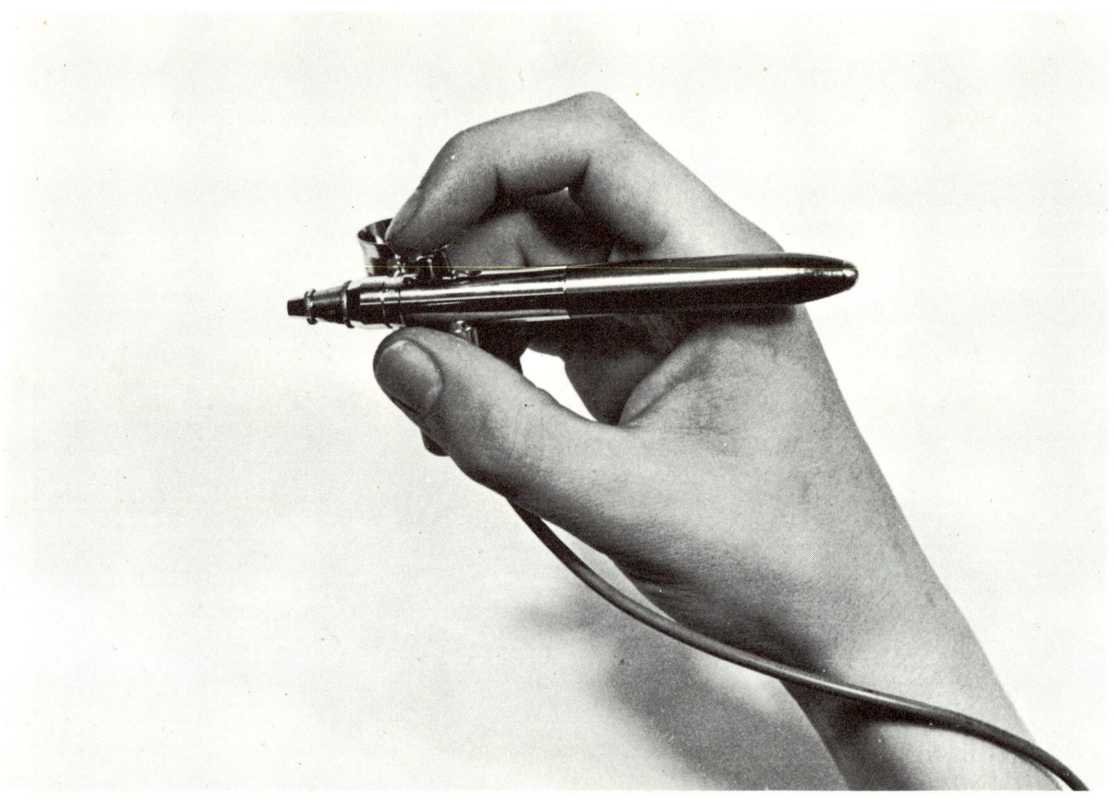

Holding a double action airbrush

specks of colour from spurting out, press gently on the air pressure button until a spray appears, and slowly but steadily, without a pause, continue past the end of the surface, keeping the wrist firm and moving the entire arm. When you have gone beyond the surface to be painted release the air pressure button. Keep your hand moving parallel throughout to prevent excessive paint build-up in any one area.

A double-action brush requires far more control and experience in co-ordinating the procedures to achieve desired finishes. First, start the hand moving before reaching the paint surface. Secondly, as the hand is moving, press down on the air release button (but no paint, yet). Thirdly, with the hand moving, and with the finger pressed down on the air release button, gently pull back on the air release button to start the paint flowing. Continue across the paint surface and beyond. As you go past the end of the surface, let the button return to its original position slowly, shutting off the paint flow, and release the button smoothly to cut off the air flow. Blobs of paint on the beginning of the paint surface indicate that paint is suddenly being released without the button being pressed down to release air or that the movements are being run together. Blobs at the end of the stroke indicate that the paint supply button is not being allowed to return forward. Specks of paint at the end indicate that the paint control has been allowed to snap forward rather than being released gradually. Constant practice is necessary to co-ordinate the movements and they should be mastered *before* attempting to paint your model.

Distance from your paint surface will depend on the pattern you are attempting. The narrower the line you seek, the closer to the paint surface you should work, with the colour control almost closed. Carefully 'draw' your line as if using a pencil. Large area coverage is achieved by opening the colour control knob and spraying from about six inches away. Always try your spray on a piece of scrap plastic before beginning a model to check for paint consistency and proper spray pattern adjustment. Since some thinners cause changes in the paint because of evaporation, it is also wise to check the spray between coats and make any needed adjustments. Drying time will vary with brands of paint but care should be taken since masking tape will pull up paint when removed unless the surface of the paint closest to the model is dry.

When starting out with airbrushing, your experimenting should, among other things, determine the drying times of your various mixes to allow proper masking. Keep notes for later reference. Remember to spray into the areas to be painted from all the edges, to prevent overspray, and then fill in the centre. For example, spray wings from the trailing edge three-quarters of the way towards the leading edge, and repeat the procedure from the leading edge. In all cases, angle your airbrush away from the fuselage, if using contrasting colour, and do not spray towards the areas of the lower colour.

Paint should never be piled onto a model in an attempt to cover the surface in a single pass. Rather, mist on the first coat by covering the entire surface to be painted with a hint of colour and allowing it to dry for a few moments. Make another pass and deepen the coverage, keeping paint from building up, and allow to dry again. Continue light coats until the desired depth of colour and coverage is achieved. An occasional build up of paint can be quickly dried by removing the colour cup, spraying out any remaining colour on a rag, and shooting air gently around the wet area, which will dry quite fast.

Your airbrushing skill should be increased by building it gradually, using more difficult schemes as you improve. The following suggested progression allows for a feeling of accomplishment and pride in your work as the more difficult techniques are mastered gradually without too many large jumps.

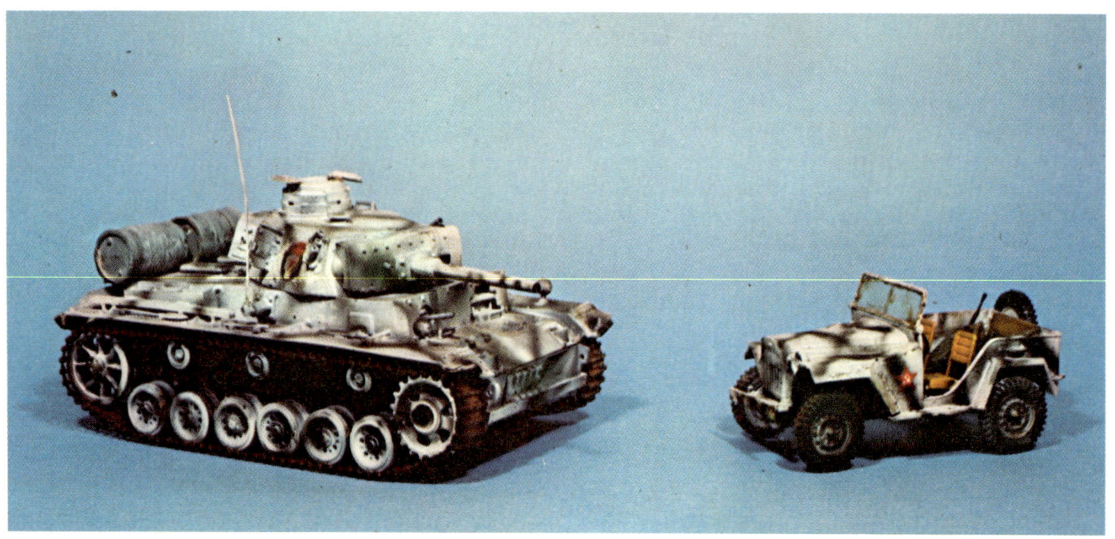

Above: The black and white winter camouflage scheme of the Russian army of World War 2 applied to a captured Panzer III and a Gaz 67B Russian jeep. (Models by Ralph Laughton).

Below: A Panzer II of the Afrika Korps in overall sand, lightly "dusted" with a lighter shade of sand to give a dusty, bleached effect (Model by Ralph Laughton).

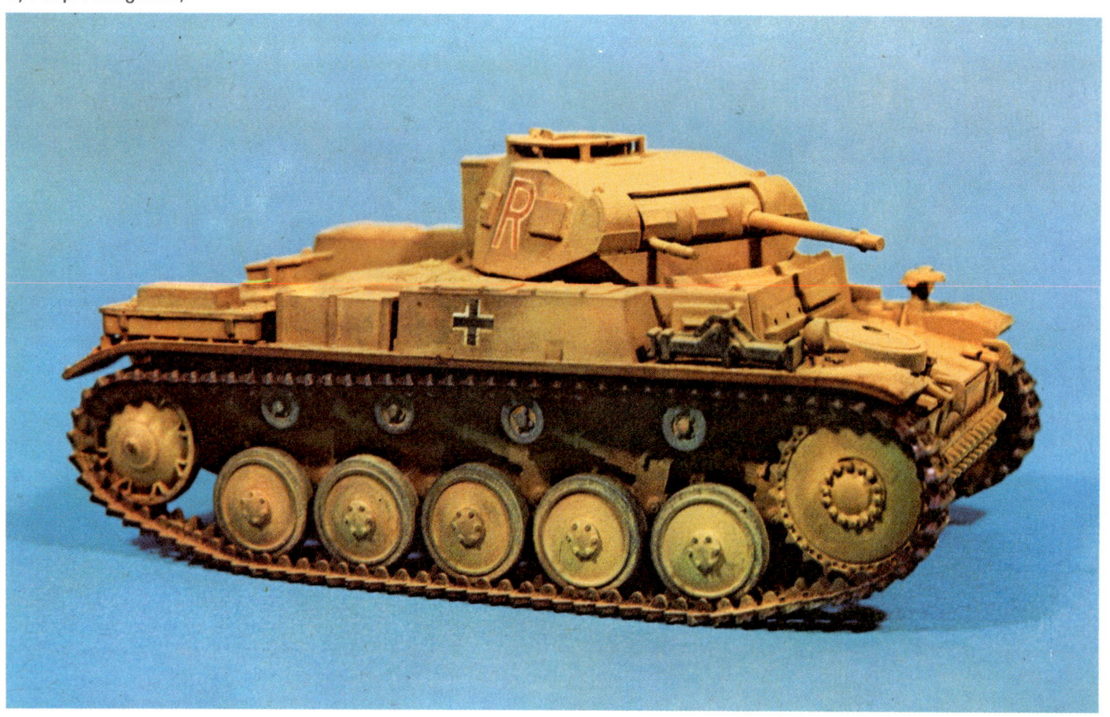

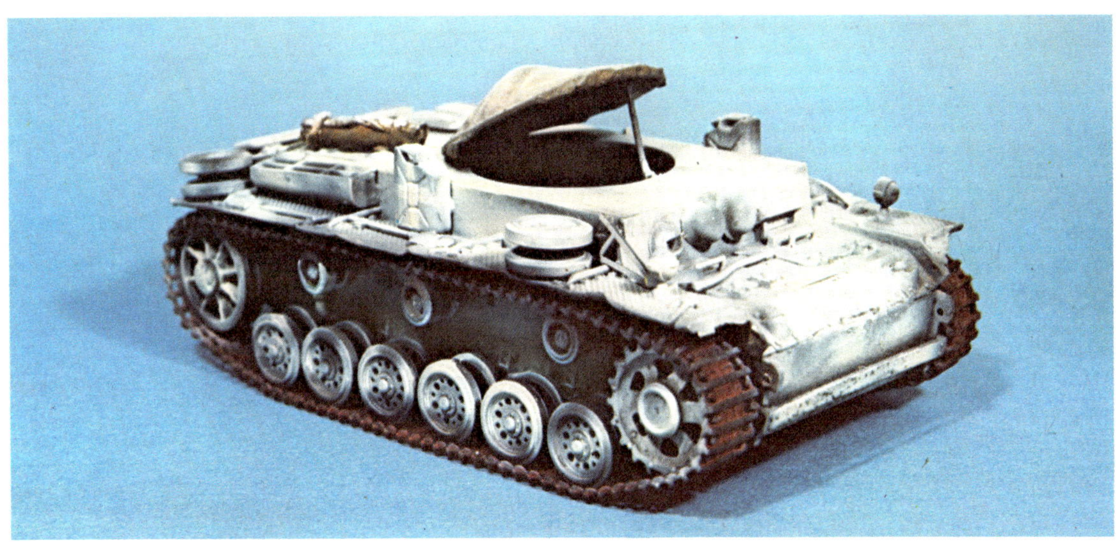

Above: A Panzer III A.R.V. hurriedly "white washed" over Panzer Grey. Note the patches of original colour showing through the "white wash" (Model by Ralph Laughton).

Below: Typical Italian/German mottled finish on an Italian command tank (Model by Ralph Laughton).

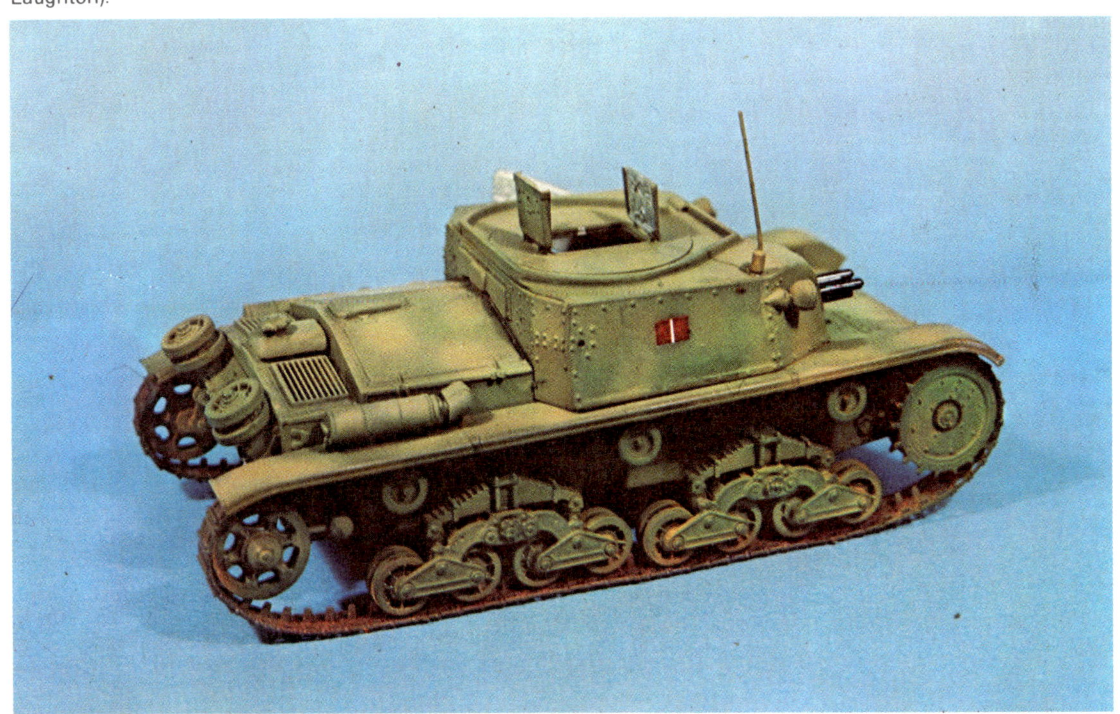

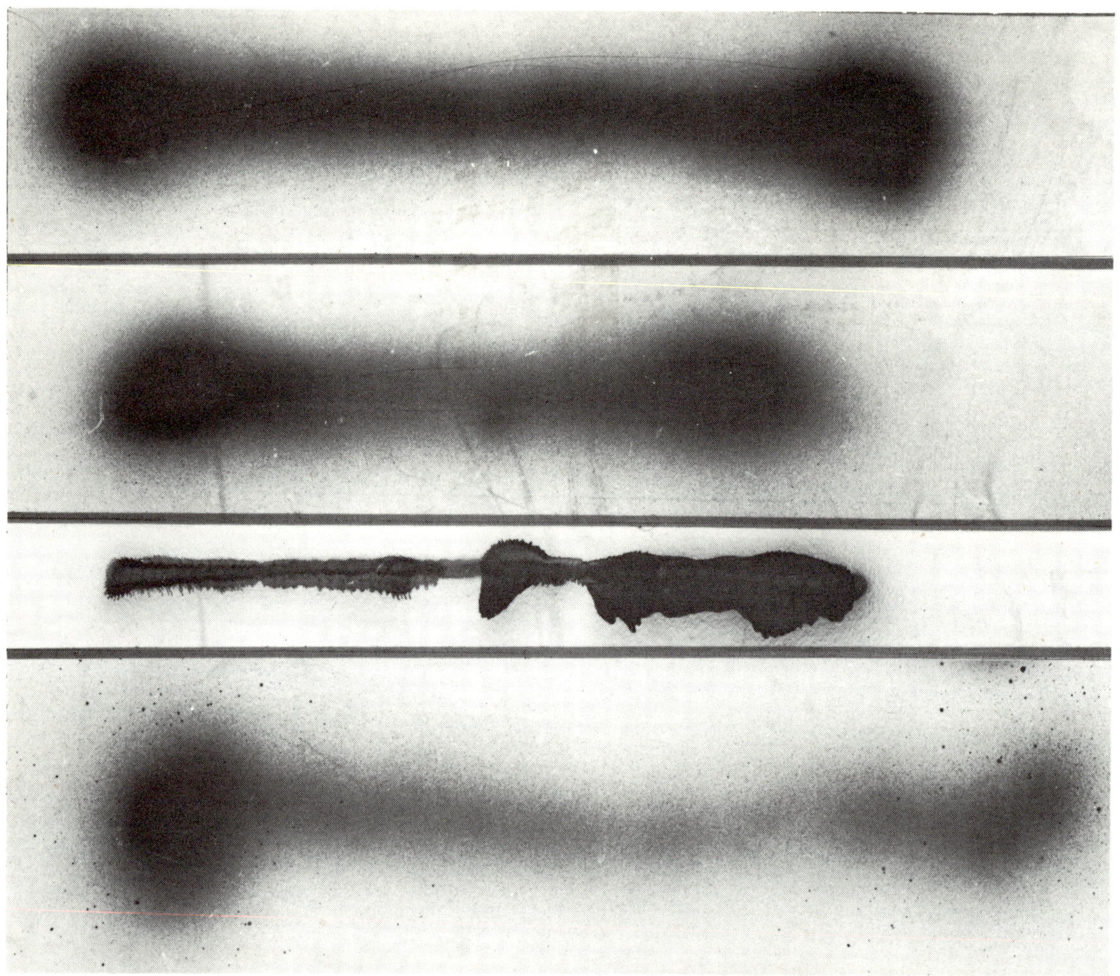

Top: If large spots of paint occur at the beginning of each stroke you are releasing the paint before the hand is in motion. If the blob is at the end, you are not allowing the finger to move forward at the end of the stroke, thus shutting off the paint supply.

Second to top: Flared strokes; This is caused by not moving the whole forearm across the model when making strokes but merely turning the wrist in order to reach the edges of the model. Make the stroke with the forearm moving across the model.

Second to bottom. Centipede Effect: This is caused by airpainting too close to the model and pulling back too far on the finger lever. If a fine line is required, work close to the model but pull back only very slightly on the finger lever; or raise the hand higher, thereby getting a broader pattern.

Bottom: Spatter; Fairly large specks of colour at the beginning of a stroke are generally caused by having allowed the finger lever to "click" forward too abruptly at the end of the previous stroke. The finger lever should be allowed to return to its normal position gently. Check for clogging.

SINGLE OVERALL COLOUR

Since overall black and overall silver have some technical problems, it is best to start with a colour which gives good coverage and is also pleasing to the eye. Glossy blue is excellent for the purpose. It contrasts well with decals, and there is a full range available of applicable late World War 2 U.S. Navy aircraft, and British schemes, as well. Additionally, many of the World War 2 U.S. aircraft were later turned over to other nations and new national markings were substituted.

Overall black, if done well, can give interesting results. Care must be taken not to allow a sameness of finish to give a dull, uninteresting appearance. If you are doing a matt finish, use different brands of flat black in various areas to give depth and variety. Highlight surfaces exposed to wear with a 'lighter' black mixture indicative of fading (see Chapter 7).

TWO COLOURS

Determine from your reference photo whether the line between the upper and lower surface colours is a hard masked one or a soft-edge. In either event, spray the lower colour first, going up the model beyond the area to be covered by the top colour to allow it to fully overlap the lower colour.

For a hard edge, use the striping tape and masking tape method, with the lower surfaces covered to prevent overspray. Plain white paper held with masking tape along critical edges will do the job.

The model should be placed in the 'no hands' box to allow freedom of spray adjustment. As you spray into the top colour area, let the back edge of the fine spray mist creep towards the tape, but not into it. The tape itself will give you a good crisp edge. After completing work close to the tape, fill in one side of the model (out of the box) with several mist coats of colour until good depth is achieved. Allow a few moments to dry, turn the model around, and repeat on other side.

After drying for about ten minutes, remove the tape *carefully* and touch up any overspray areas with your brush almost completely closed for the very finest line you can achieve. Touch up no more than what has to be sprayed to prevent a blotchy appearance. Your touch up should be an exact match of the original colour.

A soft edge between two surfaces requires no masking tape.

Place the model in the 'no hands' box as previously described. Use a file card (cut if necessary for curved surfaces) held firmly in the left hand approximately one inch from the model (closer for a harder edge, further away for a softer edge), and spray carefully over the top edge of the card to establish your line. Work carefully along one side of the model until the line is completed. Allow the back edge of the spray to work away from the newly painted line into the unpainted area, until one side is completed. Turn the model around and place it in the box, and repeat the process.

GERMAN SPLINTER CAMOUFLAGE

By combining the techniques previously discussed, masking and upper and lower colour airbrushing, you can easily proceed to the typical Luftwaffe aircraft splinter camouflage of dark green (dunkelgrun 71) and black-green (schwarzgrun 70) with light blue (hellblau 65) below. Spray the lower colour blue first, proceeding slightly up the sides of the fuselage and allow to dry. Using striping and masking tape, fix the demarcation line between upper and lower colours according to your reference photo.

Spray the lighter colour, dark green, first, since darker colours have a tendency to show through the lighter colours. Allow to dry.

When the lighter green has fully dried, follow your reference photo and mask off the light green areas *not* to be painted. Striping and masking tape patterns alone if desired, can be used. Be sure there are no uncovered gaps in your masking which will allow overspray to show. Spray black-green and allow to dry before you remove your masking. Do any touch ups with the finest possible spray with the airbrush ⅛ inch from the surface to prevent overspray.

SHADOW AND SEGMENT CAMOUFLAGE

Perhaps the most widely used of all camouflage schemes is the shadow, or segmented type (sometimes termed disruptive pattern). Follow the methods described in the chapter on Masking, using the template method for soft edges, lightly pencilling in the demarcation lines and following, but covering them as you spray. Use shaped masking tape for hard lines, as appropriate. In all cases, do your lower colour first and proceed from the lightest top colours to darkest, allowing sufficient time for drying.

U.S. NAVY THREE TONE SCHEME

In February 1943, the camouflage on all U.S. Navy aircraft carrier planes was changed from a two colour scheme of non-specular (non- reflective) blue grey above and non-specular light grey below to a scheme of non-spec white below, non-spec Sea Blue on the fuselage top surfaces, semi-gloss Sea Blue on upper wing and horizontal stabilizer, and Intermediate Blue on fuselage sides and fin and rudder. All demarcation lines were extremely soft or 'feather' edged, blending one surface well into the other. While no specific regulation has been found for World War 2 U.S. aircraft, an order of 19th. January, 1967 requires an overlap of colour of at least two feet (slightly more than 5/16 inch on a 1:72 scale aircraft). The variations were many because the official directives were somewhat vague as to the application, as opposed to colour description which was quite precise.

Proper application uses the principles previously described with the white underside being first applied. Intermediate Blue is airbrushed from the lower quarter of the fuselage side upward so that a *very* soft edge marks the joining of the two colours. This join can be done freehand with the model in the holding box if you are skilful, or by using a file card held approximately 1 inch to 1½ inches from the model and shooting over the card to give a soft edge. Variations were evident from aircraft to aircraft, as photographs clearly show. In fact, some Grumman Avenger schemes show a somewhat hard wavy demarcation line between White and Intermediate Blue. Continue the Intermediate Blue on the fin and rudder and on all upper surfaces so that blending is made easier.

After drying, airbrush 'non-spec' Sea Blue carefully along the spine and upper surfaces of the fuselage, allowing a soft spray line to blend into the Intermediate Blue. Use the file card template, if necessary to prevent overspray. Allow to dry and tape off protected areas where the wings and horizontal stabilizers join the fuselage. Be sure the masking follows the curve of the join. Spray semi-gloss Sea Blue on the wings and horizontal surfaces of the tail plane *away* from the fuselage. Gradually bring the spray (still aimed away) back towards the fuselage wing root so that the back edge of the spray fills in the area adjacent to the masking. Allow to dry and remove the masking tape which should show a crisp join of colour at the wing root area.

MOTTLE

Excellent reference sources exist depicting the use of a mottled, or soft and blurred spray of colour, effect on World War 2 aircraft and tanks. (Generally, Luftwaffe aircraft employed several fuselage colour variations, including light grey with dark grey mottle, light blue with dark blue mottle, tan with dark brown mottle, together with traditional splinter camouflage on wings and spine. The fuselage side colour was blended into the upper surface and the mottle colour was applied in a fashion to softly blend into the fuselage colour).

The mottle was not simply a blob of contrasting colour but was a soft, variable pattern of irregular blurred shapes. To achieve a good mottle finish, plan your placement prior to spraying, even to using pencil dots for spacing and location.

Practice on a scrap model with your colour flow down to its lowest point and with very gentle pressure on the air button until you find the proper distance from your model for your particular airbrush and air supply. Adjust the colour flow as necessary to obtain the proper effect. The closer to the model you hold your airbrush, the sharper will be your mottle, which should be a single puff of colour without a hard centre. Touch up as little as possible.

GERMAN WAVY BAND CAMOUFLAGE

Sometimes known as 'mirror' the continuous wavy line of light grey or light blue on top surfaces (over various under colours) of Luftwaffe aircraft is one of the most eye catching of finishes. Originally used only on aircraft operating over water, the effect was later adopted on reconnaissance aircraft such as the FW 189 in Russia and North Africa and on Hs 126 aircraft, as well.

To achieve the effect, the airbrush is used like a pen to draw a continuous wavy line of equal width over all top surfaces. Observing the size of the aircraft and the width of the lines on your research photo (the variations were considerable) begin on the outer wing and 'draw' a line with your airbrush which appears to be endless, curving and looping around in shapeless fashion until the entire wing is completed, without crossing lines. Your airbrush is working about ⅛ inch to 1/16 inch from the surface, depending on the width of your line. The pattern is a planned, though random one, which keeps a somewhat equal distance from adjacent lines. Pick up the squiggle again at the opposite wing and bring to the wing root. Plan the fuselage design and begin at the demarcation line of upper and lower colours, again looping and curving your line along and over the fuselage, until the entire body is covered. Complete by doing the fin and stabilizers in the same manner.

A random squiggle such as used on Ju88 Night Fighters and on some Me 262's is done in similar fashion, with the squiggle criss-crossing itself and looping back and forth without pattern over the fuselage surfaces.

It is important to have a good mix which dries upon hitting the surface to prevent blots and dripping which can easily spoil the effect. Go slowly and check your spray each time you stop your air flow. Also, take care that your hand, which is close to painted surfaces does not touch wet areas.

A final word of caution. Before ruining a newly finished model with a technique you have never used, take some time to try your skill and realise your problem areas. Work the schemes on scrap models until you feel confidence in your own abilities and then start in earnest.

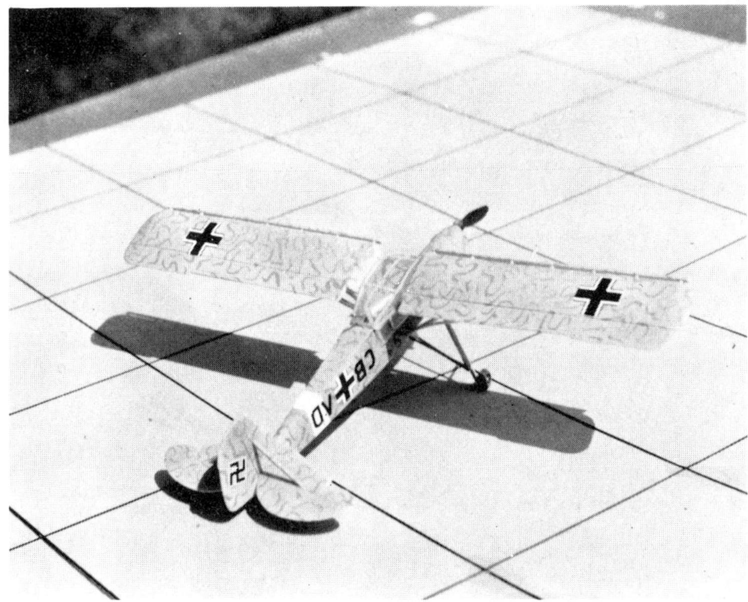

A Fieseler Fl 156 Storch (Stork) is shown in desert scheme of overall sand with a random "squiggle pattern" of light grey (Model by R. Goldman).

7: Finishing the Job

FINAL FINISH

Your model is now but a step or two away, hopefully, from your friends' admiring 'oohs' and 'ahs'. Having applied your paint scheme, permitted it to dry hard for a day and applied your decals without film surround, you are ready to complete your model with a proper finish. To ensure that your hard spent airbrush time is not wasted with decals having an 'after thought' look and to obtain an overall look of realism representing the prototype,

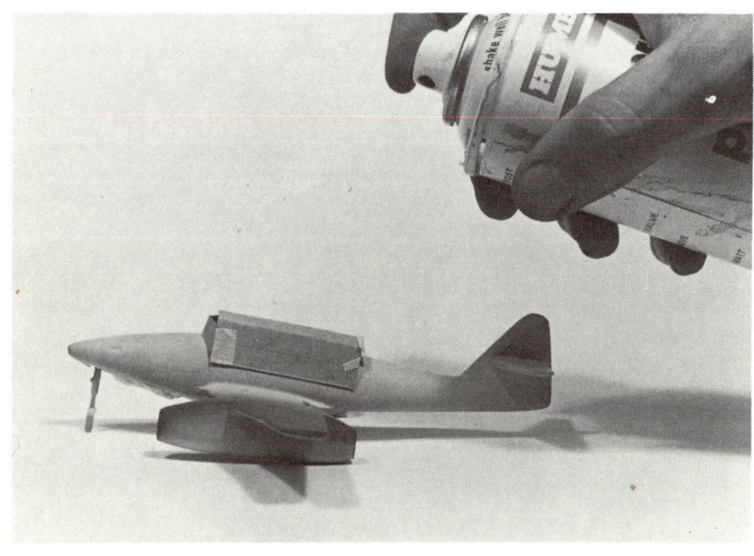

Left: A mask made from file card can be used to protect clear plastic when a finishing coat of varnish is applied.

some final steps should be taken.

Depending on your research photograph for the particular type involved, you have several choices of overall finish, matt, semi-matt (or semi-gloss ... same thing) and gloss. The purpose of each is to integrate the paint scheme and decals into one unit. Several good products are available for the purpose, and they are applied with your airbrush as you would apply paints. Others are applied directly from an aerosol spray can. Care must be taken that clear plastic areas are not sprayed as unwanted clouding will result. A simple mask of file card or liquid mask will suffice as protection so long as you keep your spray from going under it. Thin your gloss or glaze well and follow the bottle instructions. As with all airbrushing steps, try your mixture on a painted discarded model first and let dry.

If using an aerosol spray can shake well before using and apply from a distance of about ten inches in long, sweeping strokes, starting your spray away from the model and continuing without pause past the model. This prevents droplets from forming and allows several thin coats to be applied, with drying between each. Do not handle while drying or your own personal fingerprint will for ever identify your model! Rather, do the upper and side surfaces and allow to dry thoroughly, then turn the model over, propped firmly against a support, and complete spraying of the lower surfaces. The result will give the model an overall smoothness of correct finish and the decals a painted look. It will also protect the model from wear and paint chipping.

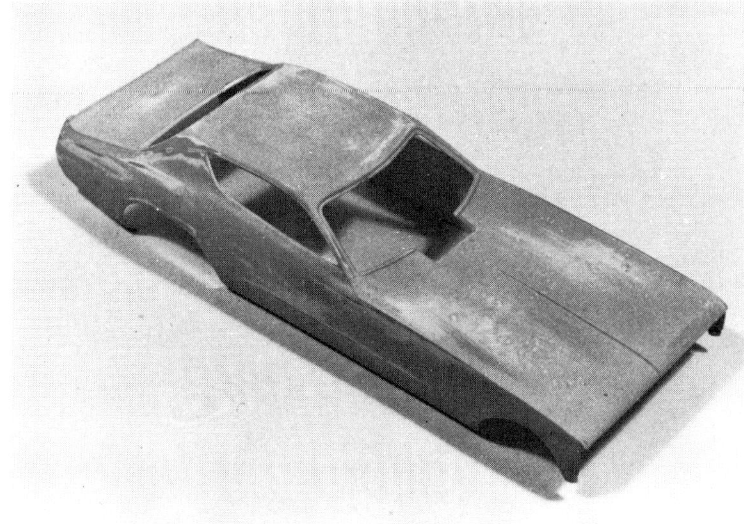

Left: When using gloss paint, use an undercoat of matt paint the same colour as your final finish. When it is dry, sand it down to give a perfect finish on which to spray your final coat.

WEATHERING

Two schools of model finishing exist, seemingly at odds, but actually quite compatible with each other. On one hand are those modellers who never build other than factory finish, museum standard models, spotless and gleaming off the assembly line. On the other side are the modellers of worn and weary, grimy and exhaust-stained models, realistic in their chipped paint and faded colours.

Somewhere, halfway between the two, is the modeller who, as an interesting scheme strikes his fancy, will do his aircraft or tank in a finish compatible with his photographs and research. He is not hide-bound to one particular school of thought but is flexible enough to gain the full enjoyment of his modelling. This type of modeller may take a factory finish some years in the display case and refinish it in weathered fashion. The model gains a feeling of having led a full operational life from production line to combat. The realism, in many cases, lends a new dimension to your modelling but care must be taken that you do not simply have a badly built model overlaid with dirt. To that end, your weathering should be planned and should resemble wear and tear shown on your research photographs.

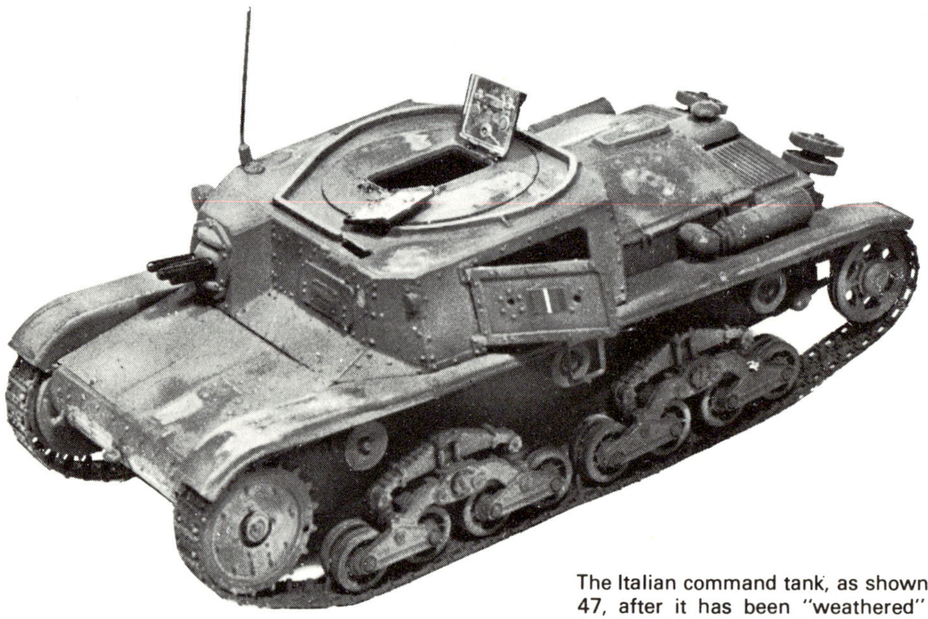

The Italian command tank, as shown in colour on page 47, after it has been "weathered" (Model by Ralph Laughton).

WEAR MARKS AND CHIPPING

Since all aircraft (except early ones covered in fabric or plywood) cars, tanks, ships, etc. are metal skinned under their paint, it is only logical that white paint 'chips' dabbed on the model are not realistic examples of paint having been chipped off heavy wear areas. The ideal worn paint area is one in which the metal under the paint shows through the worn spots.

An excellent method of depicting chipping and wearing is to give the model a metallic undercoat before applying the colour scheme. Many modellers are now doing all their models like this so that they can later be weathered, if desired. Flat silver or aluminium paint can be used but be certain that it is thoroughly dry before painting your top coat.

After overnight paint drying, lightly run the flat smoother side of a ladies' emery nail board over the areas to be chipped and worn until the silver below shows through. Some modellers prefer using a tightly wadded ball of the very finest steel wool for the wearing down. Understate the chipping and wearing and take care not to scratch your finish but rather carefully wear the paint down in the correct areas, including rivet heads which pop through paint in worn areas quite often. The abrasive grain of the nail board acts in the same manner as gravel or stones and the steel wool gives a good scuffed and worn effect. Go lightly and constantly check against overdoing the job.

FUEL STAINS

From your reference materials determine the location of the aircraft or vehicles' refuelling cap. Using a mixture of 1 drop of flat black mixed into 3-4 drops of thinner in an eye dropper, allow a drop of the mixture to fall on the fuel cap location. The resulting stain will realistically depict the over flow or runoff.

EXHAUST STAINS

If any phase of weathering can have its own individual personality, it must be the variety of shapes and locations of exhaust stains, caused by the airflow pattern. The importance of good photographic references cannot be overestimated to obtain an accurate representation of the exhaust pattern of the original you are depicting.

Following the shape, thickness and direction of staining, gently airbrush the exhaust streak in dark grey, laying on lightly with your colour control knob almost closed and your airbrush about ¼ inch to ½ inch from the model, depending on the size and scale, until the streak becomes distinct, with a slightly flared shape. Allow to dry and airbrush a soft grimy black streak the length of the stain to indicate the darker area of carbon buildup. Again, understate and refer to your photograph to prevent an exaggerated unrealistic result.

GUN PORTS

The black blast streaks which can be seen around aircraft gun ports are caused by the powdered cordite in the bullets being fired as they separate from the shell casing. The result is a spurt of black powder which is carried by airflow into a thin streak, similar to the action on exhaust stains.

Apply a very fine streak of thinned grimy flat black with your airbrush colour flow turned down to the narrowest spray from a distance of ⅛ inch to ¼ inch, depending on the scale of your model. The streak should be on both the upper and lower surfaces for wing guns (darker below due to airflow) and forward and slightly aft of the gun port on guns mounted in the cowls or in gun packs, since the blast is initially forward and then is swept slightly to the rear of the gun port by airflow. A light streak to the rear of the shell ejector ports is also appropriate.

Caution: Understate your streaks, which should be real but unobtrusive looking, and should never dominate your model. A painted on look will destroy the soft streaking which occurs and should be avoided.

BLEACHING AND FADING

The extent to which aircraft, A.F.V.'s, ships, trains, etc. fade from their original colours will depend upon the nature and extent of their exposure to the elements. Sun, sand, heat and salt water all have a fading effect on paints due to corrosion and oxidation, with upper exposed surfaces being most vulnerable. Seaplanes and flying boats particularly provide the modeller with an excellent example of fading and chipping, especially those used in tropical waters such as the Pacific where strong sun was an added factor. Once again, find a good reference photograph from which to work and avoid haphazard, unrealistic effects.

Having decided to weather your model from the outset, spray

your metal undercoat as described previously. Using a proper paint and thinner mix add white paint up to 50% of the volume of your colour (i.e. 10 drops of white to 20 drops of grey, as the case may be) depending on how faded and bleached you desire your model. Start with a 25% addition of white and experiment with increased amounts, since white can always be added, but not removed, until you achieve the desired effect. Keep notes of your mixture for later reference. Spray lightly in mist coats until the colour suits you and after drying proceed to weather and chip, keeping a cautious eye on your research photo.

If you decide to fade and bleach as an afterthought, or on a previously finished model, prepare a mixture of flat white considerably thinned down with turpentine or another thinner, to a chalky appearance. Take care not to overthin or your paint will be affected by the turpentine. Experiment on a discarded model to obtain the proper appearance of bleaching, adding white or thinner to the mix as needed.

Various water based whitewashes were sprayed over aircraft and tanks for operations in Russia. As they washed off due to wear, the undercolours showed through in a blotchy, irregular appearance. The effect can be achieved by completing your basic scheme and overspraying with a thinned down mixture of white. Follow a good photo reference and make no attempt to completely cover all areas. Rather let the undercolour show through in random fashion.

Variations of the same colour and emphasis on selected areas are required on some models for a pleasing appearance. Night-fighters in overall black, for example, have a sameness which should be broken with a 'lighter' mix of black applied to the more obvious upper surface areas. Add a few drops of white to the black paint, or use a lighter shade of grimy black, and carefully airbrush a soft spray along those areas such as the fuselage top surface, nacelles and wings where it would be more likely exposed to the sun during daylight hours.

Bleaching and fading give a particularly realistic appearance to trains constantly exposed to the sun without repainting or clean-up. Rust, grime and dirt on rolling stock also contribute to a shabby, but realistic, appearance.

DIRT AND GRIME

Modellers of A.F.V.'s and trains are particularly fond of realistic effects in their models. Those types are heavily subjected to the effects of dirt and mud from the terrain on which they operate, although factory fresh finishes can be quite realistic, as well.

Unlike aircraft, wheeled or tracked vehicles have built-in dirt and mud catchers due to the nature of their treads and wheels.

Under combat conditions A.F.V.'s receive little in the way of cleaning because the added discolourations are valued as natural camouflage. There is also little danger of overdoing them since photographs indicate that buildups of mud, rust, grime, dirt, grease, oil and other stains are commonplace. They are all deposited on the vehicles paint scheme and give an added dimension to the surface to which the modeller should direct his attention.

Having completed your model in an appropriate scheme, determine from photos the placement of your dirt and mud. Wheels and tread areas are obvious and the many angles and crevices on the hull also collect dirt. Since paint chips quickly in the tread areas from use, rust forms quickly on bogies and treads and they should be airbrushed with red oxide. The hull areas subjected to wear, around hatches and turret and footholds, should be carefully and lightly touched with rust since the constant usage will wear the rust off, as well, and not permit it to build up. Lightly spray, with your colour control almost closed, fine lines of rust down the sides of the hull for runoff from the rusted areas. The same method can be used on ships to depict rust lines on the hull and hatch areas.

Mud has a beauty of its own, as every modeller of tracked vehicles well knows. It also has a surface dimension which paint alone cannot depict. As an undercoat, one of the manufactured 'mud' paints should be sprayed over and around the tread area and upwards to the hull area. Keep in mind that mud when dried was easily dislodged and did not completely cover those areas, but did leave a residue of tannish colour.

Next, make a mixture of water and earth which has been sun-baked and has a tan, dried appearance (gather a jar full in the hot weather and keep it sealed from moisture for later use) until you have a lumpy paste. Apply liberally with a small brush **(not your airbrush)** in the tread areas and the lower hull and allow to dry out completely. The finish will be as authentic and real as can be achieved.

Lastly, dust from tanks travelling through dry areas is thrown up in clouds and settles on upper surfaces and can be realistically depicted by a spray of tan paint. Open your airbrush to a full spray and from a distance of about one foot shoot a spray of "dust" over the top of the tank allowing it to settle from the air above on top surfaces. Apply in a light mist coat or two and don't overdo.

A final word of caution of weathering: it should never be used to cover up an inadequate job of modelling under the guise of realism. Sloppy work *is* sloppy work, no matter how much chipping and wear you give it.

8: Cleaning Up

Because the opening at the tip of the airbrush through which the paint is sprayed is only a pinhole in diameter, keeping the tip, and the rest of the airbrush free of clogging debris, is essential.

After each session of airbrushing, when you are finished for the day, remove the colour cup, unhook the airbrush free from the air supply hose and unscrew the needle from the tip with gentle finger pressure. Clean the body of the airbrush with a cloth dampened with thinner, being careful to clear all paint from the hole in the air cap. A cotton swab dipped in thinner is a handy shape for the purpose. Never, but never, poke about the hole in the nozzle with a pin or knife point to remove dried pigment. This will distort the opening and cause an irregular spray, requiring the replacement of the nozzle. If the pigment refuses to loosen from the air-hole, place the airbrush tip down overnight in a jar containing enough thinner to cover the tip. A split match stick is useful to loosen dried pigment after a night's soaking.

The colour cup with the bottom removed should be flushed in brush cleaner. A pipe cleaner (cut in thirds for easy handling) run through the neck of the cup will draw out any loosened pigment and brush cleaner. Dry the cup with a facial tissue or cotton swab.

The nozzle is placed with brush cleaner in a tobacco tin. Hold the nozzle up to the light and, if cleaned completely, a circle of light will show through. If not, repeat the process, soaking overnight if necessary. The colour adjusting part tip is cleaned in the same manner.

Reassemble the airbrush after cleaning off dried paint from all threaded parts.

It often happens in an airbrushing session that all factors are

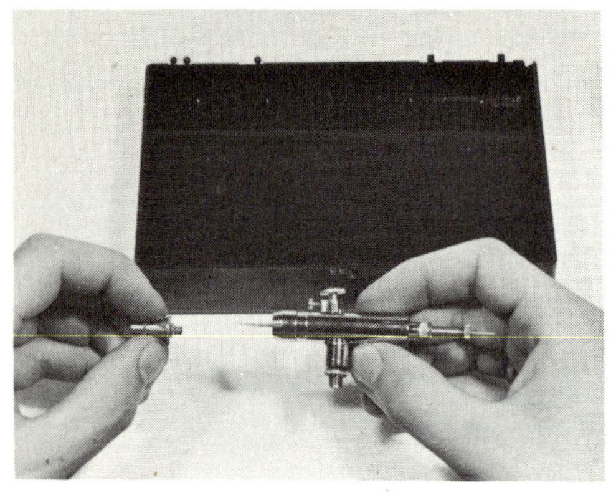

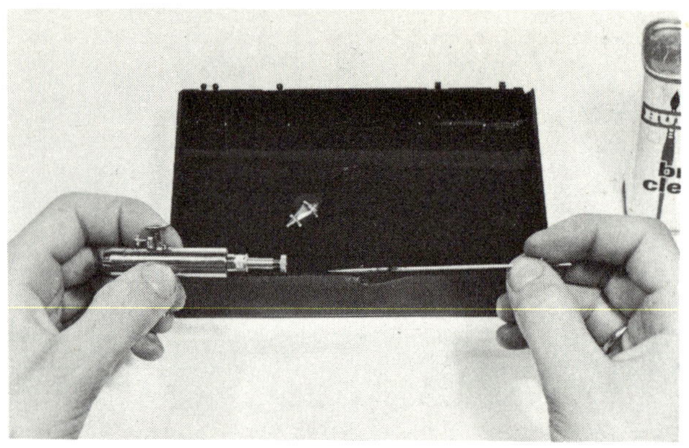

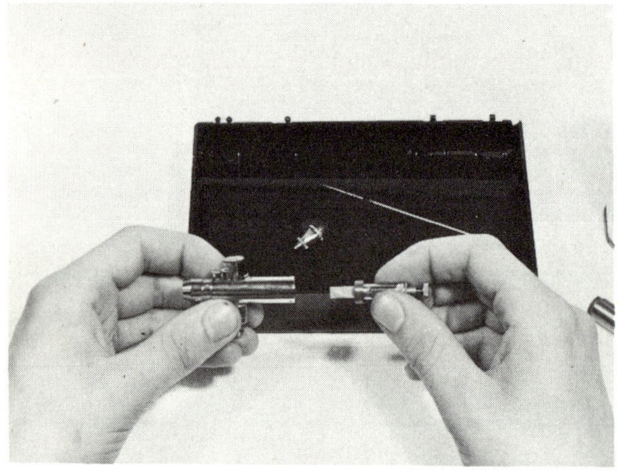

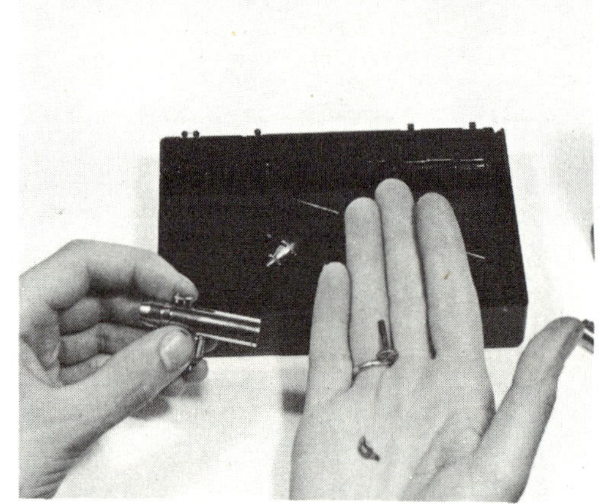

Step by step method of dismantling a double action airbrush, in this case the Badger 100 IL|XF, for cleaning.

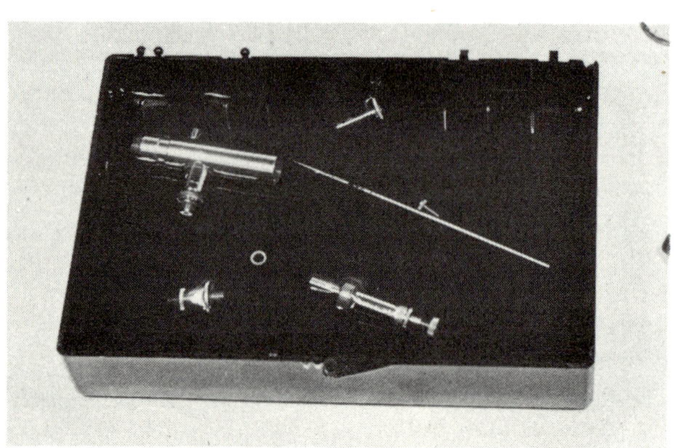

in perfect harmony — your hand is steady as a rock, your paint mixes are perfect, the mixture is drying on contact, etc, and the last thing you want to do is stop to break down your airbrush for cleaning before changing colours. A fast cleaning method (admittedly not as thorough as a final cleaning, for which it is not a substitute) is to switch colour cups, letting the first cup soak in a jar of brush cleaner. Then, using an eyedropper shoot a jet of thinner into the opening into which the colour cup neck fits and press down on the finger control button, forcing thinner through the needle out the airhole and into a cleaning rag.

Repeat the procedure until the thinner comes through absolutely clear. Then, fill the new clean colour cup with thinner, attach to the colour opening and flush the cupful of thinner through the airbrush. In a matter of a minute or two your brush is ready for a fresh colour, preferably darker than the first in case a speck of the old colour is still in the brush. Never use white as your second colour, with this method since it will pick up even the most minute specks of a darker colour. On occasion, three colour changes can be done with this way if the colours are compatible in shading. Be sure all thinner is completely flushed through before applying the new colour to your model to prevent splattering a residue of thinner on your paint surface.

Occasionally, your airbrush may clog while working due to a particle of paint being caught in the needle or in the airhole tip. Often it can be jarred loose by placing the tip of the finger over the air hole opening and pressing down on the finger control button. This will force air into the airhole where the tip of the finger will force the air back through the needle, dislodging (hopefully) the particle of paint and forcing it back into the colour cup. It should then be removed to prevent a recurrance, either by using a clean colour cup or replacing the old paint. Frequent clogging may indicate that the needle is due for a full cleaning or that your paint mixture is too thick.

A double action airbrush is cleaned in the same fashion, except that the needle is removed carefully so as not to bend the tip and thoroughly cleaned with thinner. Gentle loosening of the needle with a small pair of pliers may be necessary if paint has been allowed to dry in the brush for a period of time. Flush out the brush by shooting a jet of thinner with an eye dropper directly into the opening in the side of the airbrush. Clean all parts carefully, particularly those adjacent to the needle, to allow smooth working of the air and colour control lever. Apply a dab of petroleum jelly periodically to ensure free action.

Your airbrush is an important investment and should be treated accordingly. Bad maintenance is the greatest cause of poor results, bar none, and all the skill in the world will not overcome a clogged or dirty airbrush.

Appendix

The following chapters of the International Plastic Modellers Society are listed at their last known address. Up to date information may indicate some changes.

IPMS Australia	86 Moreton Cres, Lundoora, Victoria, 3083
IPMS Austria	Vienna 1210, Nordmang 11-13/4/6, Austria
IPMS Belgium	Allee des Moutons 136, 1020 Bruxelles
IPMS Brazil	Rua Arquius Cordeiro 3165502, Meier Guanabara Rio, Brazil
IPMS Canada	P.O. Box 626, Station B, Ottowa, Ontario, Canada.
IPMS Denmark	Rebaek Sopark 5, Vaer 335, 2650 Hvidore
IPMS Finland	PO Box 798, 00101 Helsinki 10
IPMS France	c/o M. Ehrengardt, 1 Rue Carnot 93, Gagny, France.
IPMS Germany	1000 Berlin 37, Oertzenweg 12 B, W. Germany
IPMS Iceland	c/o B. Magnusson, Hraunbae 134, Reykjavik
IPMS Italy	Casella Postale 12017, 0010 Roma, Belsito, Italy
IPMS Netherlands	c/o D.A. Van Eck, Irenelaan 26, Soest, Netherlands
IPMS Norway	c/o Knut Arveng, Baglerfaret 4, Oslo 6, Norway
IPMS Philippines	c/o A. Anido, PO Box 2019, Manila, D-406
IPMS S. Africa	6 Lorite. 25 Chelmsford Rd, Durban, Natal, Rep. of S. Africa
IPMS Sweden	Onskevadersgatan 47, S-41735 Goteborg, Sweden
IPMS Switzerland	Werdstrasse 121, 8003 Zurich, Switzerland
IPMS U.K.	P. Clisby, Flat 8, Peabody Estate, Hammersmith, London W6 9QW.
IPMS U.S.A.	PO Box 163, Ben Franklin Station, Washington, D.C. 20044